DOWNSHIFTING

DOWNSHIFTING

The ultimate handbook

ANDY BULL

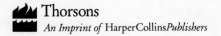
Thorsons
An Imprint of HarperCollins*Publishers*

Thorsons
An Imprint of HarperCollins*Publishers*
77–85 Fulham Palace Road,
Hammersmith, London W6 8JB

Published by Thorsons 1998
10 9 8 7 6 5 4 3 2 1

© Andy Bull 1998

Andy Bull asserts the moral right to
be identified as the author of this work

A catalogue record for this book
is available from the British Library

ISBN 0 7225 3566 X

Printed and bound in Great Britain
by Creative Print and Design (Wales), Ebbw Vale

Dedicated to Elena, Beatrice and Fred, and to my mother

CONTENTS

ACKNOWLEDGEMENTS

I am greatly indebted to all those downshifters and would-be downshifters who have allowed me to tell their stories in this book.

Many individuals and organisations gave me valuable assistance, in particular the *New Ways to Work* charity. I am also grateful to Geraint Price for his help with research and interviewing.

ANDY BULL

INTRODUCTION

What Is Downshifting?

The trouble with the rat race is, even if you win you are still a rat.

CHER

Does this sound like you?

You are a success. You have the big job, the nice house, the company car and the affluent lifestyle. Congratulations. You've made it. You must be really happy.

No? Well, why not? You have, after all, spent the first half of your working life getting to where you are today. There have been sacrifices, certainly. If you are a man, you have probably allowed the demands of work to take precedence over the emotional needs of your family. You haven't seen nearly enough of the children. In fact, you sometimes feel as if you are totally missing out on the pleasures of seeing them growing up. If you are a woman, you may have sacrificed having a family at all in order to forge ahead in your career. For both sexes, relationships may well have suffered, marriages ended in divorce.

And the pressures have taken their toll. The stress and the overwork have been hard to bear at times. But they have been worth it – haven't they? After all, you can look at all you have achieved, at the approval of your parents, partner and peers, at the impact you have made on your profession, at all the staff you have brought on and who look up to you, at the products you have created, or the growth you have brought to your company – and say, with total justification, that you have truly made your mark.

So why is it all so meaningless?

Is it because the knowledge has been dawning on you over the last couple of years that there are more important things in life than clinching the next big deal, or climbing the next rung up the corporate ladder? That helping yourself so effectively has given you no time to help others? That in concentrating on being focused you have also become narrow and shallow?

Does it perhaps also have something to do with the fact that, when you are objective about it, you realise that you cannot keep up this pace of work for ever? That you know that, these days, there is no such thing as job security, or a job for life? That all your efforts, the fact you have put your job before everything else, will not mean a thing when the company comes to downsize, get lean and mean or whatever other euphemism they choose for making people redundant?

Perhaps you have watched it happen to others. Maybe you have seen the generation before yours reach the top – and then get chopped. Maybe you have noted the statistics – that 600,000 white collar jobs have been lost in the United Kingdom over five years and that it is men in their thirties and forties who are most likely to be made redundant.

But even if all this does worry you profoundly, can you get out of the trap? Even if you decide that your job is not only meaningless, damaging to your heath, your relationships with your partner and family AND that it could also be taken away from you in the not too distant future, is there any realistic alternative?

The ultimate handbook

What, in short, can you do about it?

Well, you can complain a lot, discuss it endlessly with your friends and those colleagues you trust, and then keep on in the same old rut.

Or, you can work to change your life radically for the better.

You can set about, in a carefully structured and practical way, exchanging the lifestyle of an affluent high-achiever for a life where the financial rewards are far less but the satisfaction is far greater: *downshifting*, in a nutshell.

Of course, it's by no means easy. It takes a great deal of courage and commitment to move from enjoying the daydream of downshifting to actually doing it – perhaps working for yourself, finally doing with your life what you always wanted to do but rejected for the sake of security.

But hold on a minute. Isn't it just those qualities – your courage and commitment – that got you where you are today? Why not use them now to achieve a different goal?

There will be many sacrifices – sacrifices that you may decide, after careful reflection, you are not prepared to make.

But, if you have the will, it can be done. And this book will tell you exactly how.

Downshifting will provide a structured alternative to a high-powered, high-earning career. It will tell you how to adjust, how to live on much less and how to use your newly-won spare time to do the things that really matter to you – whatever they are, from taking a degree to working for charity, from learning a new craft or skill that will open up a new career to devoting your time to your local community.

It will provide each person who reads it with a framework for re- shaping their lives in a way which suits them personally. It will cover every aspect of this fundamental change.

It is for people who have clearly made it, who have achieved many of their professional ambitions but who may

What Is Downshifting?

well have decided that those ambitions were misplaced and no longer have any allure: people who want a new and more meaningful challenge.

It is an empowering book, a book which offers a positive choice for a new life and which shows, through practical advice often drawn from those who have downshifted themselves, just how to do it.

It will give a new shape to the next phase of your life. Many people make resolutions for the New Year. With this book you can mark out the biggest resolution you will ever make – the resolution to carve out a new life for yourself in the new century.

CHAPTER ONE

I Have a Dream...

EVERYONE has their breaking point. Sooner or later everyone reaches it. People who have downshifted can usually point to a crunch time – a moment at which they decided that, however long it took, whatever the risks and the hardships, they had to downshift.

Take, for instance John Cleave, who until the age of 34 was a policeman in Bristol. His decision to downshift came one night when he was working with the drug squad.

'We picked up a prostitute,' he told me. 'She was wearing only a basque under her anorak and was in a really sorry state – sores on her legs, broken teeth and a black eye. But the thing that really got me was that she was seven months' pregnant.

'Dealing with society at its worst all the time was grinding me down. The first thing I did when I got in from work was wash my hands.

'I'd been with the police for eight years, was earning around £14,500 and had passed my sergeant's promotion exams. But disillusionment was growing and I used to think: "Why am I involved in the seedier, nastier side of life, when I could be doing something different?"'

For Fiona Aitken, who had worked as an accountant with Coopers and Lybrand for five years, the crunch came with the unexpected death of her father. As she, her mother and her five younger sisters drew together in grief she realised that the successful, secure career she had carved out as a respected senior auditor with the company did not fill the void she felt in her life. 'My father's death made me realise that life is unpredictable and precious,' she said. 'I wanted to enjoy every single day, contributing to it and getting something out of it, not just plodding on in a job I hated for the security and stability I had conned myself into believing it gave me.'

For Peter Mantle, director of a financial publishing company, the moment came when he collapsed on a business flight between Milan and Rome. 'I couldn't move my arms and legs,' he says. 'I thought I must be having a brain haemorrhage, but doctors checked me out and said, "There's not much wrong with you, except you smoke too much, you drink too much and you work far too hard." It happened three times in all. Looking back I guess this was a subconscious motivator in getting out.'

For Lisa Nelson, the decision to downshift was not particularly dramatic – it occurred one weekend when she and her husband were looking after five deprived children – but it was profound. She decided that, in spending nine years of her life building up a PR company with a turnover of £1 million a year, she had neglected what she really wanted to do with her life. She wanted to help disadvantaged children. And she wanted a family of her own. So she closed the company down.

For Tim King, a barrister, the crunch came when he was representing a group of new age travellers accused of stealing a generator. He was already disillusioned with the law, and had lost his respect for judges and his colleagues at the bar.

As a barrister, Tim earned £40,000 a year, ate out five nights a week, had a massive mortgage and great career prospects. The travellers – Wicksy, Andrew and Louise – lived on a bus and were penniless.

'I felt nothing but envy for them,' Tim remembers. 'I got them off with a caution and asked where they were headed next. Part of me thought how great it would be to join them. If I'd had the guts I'd have got up and left there and then. I hadn't, but I did decide there and then that I must carve out a new life for myself.'

These five people, in very different jobs, levels of affluence and family circumstances, all had their own, distinct ambitions, their own personal reasons for wanting to downshift. But they also had something very fundamental in common: a profound dissatisfaction with their lot and a determination that, somehow, they would change their lives for the better.

There are many tens of thousands of people in Britain who are just like them.

People who have decided that a high salary and standard of living, earned through a demanding and fulfilling job, are no compensations for long hours spent away from home and family, for stress, illness and the fear of early death. No compensation for the lack of a partner, or children.

Many who are seriously considering downshifting are often doing so because of a change in the culture of the workplace for the middle classes. Where once the professions could more or less count on a job for life, now they cannot.

I Have a Dream...

The result has been a national mood of anxiety.

Once the British middle classes were steady people choosing steady jobs and working steadily towards their pensions. Nowadays they are unsteady people. There are no certainties. Jobs for life are increasingly being replaced by short-term contracts. The trend is for large organisations to shed their salaried, full-time staff and to replace them with freelance individual suppliers.

This is the reality, increasingly, for millions of people.

We are witnessing the beginning of the end of the age of mass organisation, a process in which all of the old professional certainties are being decimated. The organisations we worked for were once secure environments which also provided a sense of camaraderie and community. Not any more.

Downshifting means coming to terms with life without the protection of a large organisation around you. Being able to do so is the key to survival in the coming world of work.

Business psychologist John Nicholson says: 'The man or woman who does not need the trappings of a large corporation around them, who is willing to find a niche in the market, and to change careers several times during the course of their working lives, will flourish in this decentralised world. Small will be beautiful, believe me.'

The new relationship at work is forcing insecure employees to work much harder because of a fear that, otherwise, they may lose their jobs. Nowhere in Europe is the situation worse than in Britain. British people work the longest average working week in the European Union. Sixteen per cent work more than 48 hours a week, and three out of four British men work 40-hours plus a week, compared to the European average of one in four. Almost 50 per cent of the British workforce report coming home feeling totally exhausted, compared with 36 per cent in the US and 17 per cent in Holland.

In a survey of 1,250 managers published recently in the *Financial Times*, almost half said that although work took priority over everything else in their lives, they would like to spend more time with family and friends. This survey shows the extent of the extra burden that has fallen on managers in recent years. Workloads for one in five managers have increased by more than 15 hours a week in just two years.

The survey found that two-thirds of managers want to work fewer hours. Ideally, 30 per cent of all employees would like to work 30 hours or less, and a fifth would like to work under 20 hours.

The white collar Manufacturing, Science and Finance Union surveyed 14,000 workers and found that 60 per cent were suffering from stress. In the 400 workplaces surveyed, workers said performance-related pay, increased workloads and 'vicious' management techniques added to stress.

Working such long hours in conditions of stress and insecurity naturally affects the whole of a person's life. There is less time for relationships with partners, friends, the family, less time for the home, for sports, hobbies and other interests.

There is also less time to do the things that middle-class people once did which were so essential to holding the fabric of the community together. Middle-class people have traditionally been the mainstays of district, town and parish councils, for example. They have sat as magistrates and as school governors, they have run youth or sports clubs and Guide, Scout, Brownie and Cub packs. Today there is a desperate shortage of volunteers in all of these areas, brought on – I suggest – not because of a decline in the sense of community, but by the ever-increasing demands at work.

It is no exaggeration, therefore, to say that the way we are forced to work is not just damaging us and our families, it is also whittling away at the fabric of the communities in which we live. How many acts of petty vandalism, for instance, might be prevented if there were the volunteers to run a youth club for bored teenagers?

There is other strong statistical evidence of a desire to reduce the pressures of work in exchange for a more fulfilling home life – and not just in Britain. The same is true for all developed nations.

In 1994 an American Gallup poll, for example, found that a third of all Americans – an unprecedentedly high figure – would take a 20 per cent cut in income if they or their spouses could work fewer hours.

In Britain, the Henley Centre for Forecasting has done a lot of research into attitudes to work. When they posed the statement 'The pace of life is too fast for me nowadays' they found widespread agreement, and discovered that the percentages agreeing with the statement went up between 1990 and 1994. Although dissatisfaction was expressed throughout the social classes, and was highest among C1s (at 40 per cent). ABs – those with the most skilled, rewarding and well-remunerated jobs – also showed high levels of dissatisfaction: 32 per cent in 1994.

Underpinning many people's decision to downshift is the fear of redundancy.

During the 1990s, hundreds of thousands of employees in the computer industry, banking, teaching, academia and the media have had to face up to redundancy. The list has included Shell, BT, Rumbelows, Norwich Union, Thorn EMI, Mercury Communications, all the High Street banks and Railtrack.

Department of Employment figures show that men under the age of 45 make up the largest number of those made redundant in Britain, and are twice as likely to lose their jobs as women.

Faced with these statistics, many people are deciding that they must prepare to downshift now, while the decision and the timing of it are theirs. Of course, if voluntary redundancy packages are on offer, they can be the key to unlock a new life with far fewer financial worries.

When such packages are offered they are routinely oversubscribed. Drake Beam Morin, the outplacement specialists, found that 30 per cent of Britons would be willing to accept voluntary redundancy if the appropriate incentives were offered.

In 1992, IBM decided to reduce drastically its staffing levels world-wide. Employees keen to take a substantial cash package and to strike out on their own flocked to take up the company's offer. In the US, 32,000 – 60 per cent more than expected – took the money. In Britain, where staffing levels were cut from 18,400 to 9,200 in the five years from 1990 to 1995, almost all left voluntarily – and well before the usual retirement age. Payoffs were substantial, around £60,000 for a middle manager on £40,000 a year. Some knew they could walk into other well-paid jobs, but many others opted for a simpler, less pressured life.

With the increasing insecurity of employees, the social contract between them and their bosses has been broken. Without unions to fight for them, and with the political and social environment turned unsympathetically Darwinian, workers – especially managers and professionals with a bit of a nest egg and a sense of emotional and intellectual security – are starting to withhold the one bargaining chip they have left – their time.

Faced with the modern reality of work as a jungle, many are concluding that downshifting is their best revenge!

Which is all very well, but where do you begin? How do you turn the dream of downshifting into a reality that works for you, that suits your needs? And, perhaps even more fundamentally, are you cut out for the challenges of downshifting?

I Have a Dream...

Certainly those who downshift tend to share certain qualities. They are resourceful, optimistic, prepared to take a risk and to rise to a challenge. But they also need a realistic sense of their aptitudes and abilities. A pure risk-taker is likely to fail just as surely as someone who hates the thought of taking any risks at all. Do you fit the profile? Ultimately, only you can decide, though this book will help you to reach the correct conclusion by asking you all the right questions and inviting you to come up with honest answers.

Of course, taking the decision to downshift is quite distinct from actually doing it. As I said, everyone who has done it has been through a crunch time when they realised that to downshift was essential and inevitable. But where you go from there, and the pattern for working to put that decision into effect, will be different with every individual.

The people I have used as case studies in this and in subsequent chapters are all working towards their own personal solutions.

Good groundwork – working towards downshifting, preparing for it, deciding what you will do, how you will re-order your life – is vital. This is something else this book will help you with.

You will, after all, be changing not just your job but your whole life. You will be reviewing not just your work and your level of income, you will be deciding where to live and what luxuries to give up; you will be forging a new future for yourself and, if you have them, your dependents. Downshifting may affect where your children go to school – whether they go through the state or private system perhaps – and hence their whole future. You will be totally restructuring your life, and your partner will be restructuring his or hers. Downshifting is a joint – or family – decision.

In the course of researching the subject I have discovered that many people share the dream of downshifting.

The ultimate handbook

Many more think it is a great idea – in theory – but can't imagine taking the plunge for themselves. I hope that, through the many and varied case studies in this book, I can help make downshifting an achievable reality for many more people who are dissatisfied with their lot.

Everyone's dream is different.

By no means do all want their own business, although many do. Not everyone wants to move out of the city to the country or to a small town, although that plays a part in the dreams of many. Some go abroad, others stay in the homes they already have or move to cheaper ones in the same locality.

Some are not merely swapping employment for a business of their own or straightforward self-employment, they are building up a portfolio of jobs, a range of money-earning skills which dovetail with a range of other activities that they do for their own enjoyment or for the benefit of others. To use the jargon, they create 'portfolio careers' for themselves.

Alexis Hallam, a consultant psychologist with Career Analysts Ltd in central London, says: 'The portfolio career is the way of the future for many people. You work a bit like a consultant. You may do several different types of work. You anchor yourself on something key, which brings home the bacon. Then you develop other themes.

'Information technology has wiped out entire tiers of middle managers. Which is why we have had so many bank managers in here recently. We find that people who have joined an organisation for one reason are now being forced to take on an entirely different type of role. We get a lot of lawyers who took up the law for reasons of truth and justice, but who say that is not what it is about any more. Now the market is so competitive, many people are being required to be sales-oriented. A lot of senior partners from law firms find they are really being asked to be sales directors.'

I Have a Dream...

Many who downshift are taking advantage of the attitudes of the (so far small) number of more enlightened employers who realise that, to keep their best people, or to attract some of the most skilled people in the market, they must offer working hours and conditions which do not conflict with the growing desire to have a rich personal or family life as well. There is even a charity, New Ways to Work, which campaigns among employers to extend flexible working arrangements (commonplace among certain lower skilled jobs) to management positions. New Ways to Work argues for the need for more sophisticated strategies to reconcile the often conflicting demands of work and family life. They lobby for the growth of techniques such as job-sharing; career breaks during which an employee can gain further qualifications, pursue outside interests or raise a young family; for reduced hours, term-time working and working from home. All of which, the charity argues, are perfectly possible for successful managers if they have an enlightened employer.

Already, major employers – including Rover Group, Lucas Industries, Boots the Chemist, the National Westminster Bank, the Inland Revenue and a number of county councils – have recognised the wisdom of this approach and are pioneering flexible working schemes for their employees. We will look at this development in detail.

But, however they do it, all who downshift have one thing in common: They are all lowering their expectations about what they can get out of their jobs – even if a lucky few end up richer than they were before! They are putting their emotional investment into values and lifestyles that depend less on work and money. Theirs is a distinctly different value system. One that is not career-centred, but focused rather on helping themselves, their families, and others. It has quality of life, not affluence, at its core.

Here is how the five people I introduced at the start of this chapter put their decisions to downshift into practice:

John Cleave spent many months looking for the right opportunity, following the decision he made after his harrowing night with the drug squad. That opportunity came one Christmas when he was visiting his parents in his old home town of Port Isaac, Cornwall, and heard that the local post office was for sale.

It was in an old lifeboat house in the most picturesque of settings on the edge of a cliff overlooking the harbour. I'd always said what a good living it could make, and when we got home to Bristol, we sat in the front room and said: 'Let's go for it.'

We'd reached a watershed in life, and the shop was the catalyst to change everything: to move somewhere nice and work for ourselves.

There was no agonising, the opportunity seemed perfect. I kept remembering: 'This is life, not a dress rehearsal.' We sold our house in Bristol for £40,000, borrowed from relatives and the bank and just managed to scrape together the £117,500 we had to pay for the property.

It was a gamble taking on this place. More by luck than judgement it has been a success. We both found we had a flair for display and for ordering nice things for the shop, and that is where we are concentrating our efforts. The post office is just steady, and we might give that side up one day.

We are in a position to do a lot of things within the community, and we do. I am honorary secretary of the lifeboat and the captain of the cricket team, my wife Caroline is the chairwoman of the play group, she has been

I Have a Dream…

chairman of the Friends of the school. And, of course, as
we run the post office we are at the centre of village life.

We made the break for our own self-respect. My
contemporaries were saying 'I don't want to lose my
pension' and that sort of thing when they had only done
seven or eight years in the police, and they were in their
late twenties and early thirties. I think that is pathetic.
It's a life sentence they are committing themselves to.
You'd get less for murder.

If at the end of the day everything turned to rat shit
and no one came into the shop, we went bust and were
kicked out into the cold, we could at least say we have
done it.

We wanted to do it, we have done it and we have
learned. We both fervently believe any experience in life
– be it good or bad – is positive.

I don't think what we have done is for everybody,
though. Some people will do things and some won't.
Some take decisions, some shy away. Some won't even
consider change. But, as a couple, change has never
bothered us. Change will happen anyway, so you can
either sit and wait for it or say, 'Hang on, let's change it
ourselves and in the direction we would like to take.'

If you want to do something else, my advice is to
just take a deep breath and jump.

Fiona Aitken had come to loathe the career-centred value system she had forced herself to create. She had gone
her own way at university, studying Anglo-Saxon and
Old High German. 'But then,' she says, 'I took the "sensible" decision to qualify as an accountant. If you're a
blonde girl, a professional qualification does at least
force people to take you seriously. Otherwise, they just
assume you're dippy.'

The ultimate handbook

I had five years of hard labour at Coopers and Lybrand. All I ever saw of the world outside was the entrance to the Tube station. I was driven to the point of collapse by pressure at work and the petty frustrations of serpentine office politics, which often continued in the all-male chumminess of the pub after hours. I just don't fit into a corporate structure.

After five years Pa was very ill and then he died and that was the catalyst for me. Life is too damn short and he died very young. How long do you want to go on commuting two hours this way, two hours that way and then all you are dying to do while at work is get home? It's not satisfying.

It was long hours and studying for exams every evening and weekend. You are either studying or feeling guilty because you are not studying. It's a slog.

I always try to buck the trend. I'm not a big corporate person. I didn't like being a cog in a wheel. I felt strait-jacketed. I don't like being told what to do. I prefer feeling I'm responsible for myself.

I left Coopers in the summer of 1994. I was in complete and utter flux. Dad had died six month earlier and I was dealing with his estate and taking decisions about my five younger sisters – where to keep this one at school, that one at university. Mum and I were darting down to see the youngest at school every weekend as she fought through her grief and pain.

It was very difficult. It was like a whirlwind had hit us and then we had to start from scratch with absolutely nothing – not even money for food – and wondering how do we exist from day to day?

It was a nightmare. I look back and I have blanks, for months at a time, when I can't remember what I did. It is like your mind blanks it out.

I knew I had to find something to do to make money. I used to walk round and round Harvey Nichols and then I suddenly thought 'What do they sell on their ground floor? Obviously their best-selling things.' All the silk shirts and scarves and stuff like that. I thought I must be able to do that. That was the starting point, focusing on what I thought I could make and sell, because I'm not a fashion designer, I don't have the training. Then I used to spend hours in the Victoria and Albert Museum because they have all the history of the fabrics and the colours, and I could work out what colours suited people with a pale English complexion.

And then I thought, I've got a family with all these sisters, we have a lot of girlfriends, and a lot of female contacts, and the whole thing started gelling. I thought that if I could make good clothes at a reasonable price and sell them through word of mouth then I would be really on to something.

So in March 1995 I launched a company called Azur. I design, manufacture and distribute clothes and accessories all over the country, through sales agents who model and sell the clothes at home or at private parties and charity fairs. In the first nine months, 85 people came to work for me.

I was able to use the financial acumen I had built up in my career, and was easily able to persuade the bank to give me a loan in order to start the company.

But I was leaping into a world I didn't know. If I had tried doing it the conventional way, knocking on the door of a company and asking for a job, they would have said go away and get some experience. I'd have had to go to fashion school, learn pattern cutting and everything like that. I'd have maybe been apprenticed as a buyer somewhere.

The ultimate handbook

I had to find suppliers, designers, pattern cutters – the whole lot. I don't sell through shops but through entrepreneurial women who I have found through friends of friends. I have around 200 but I'm aiming for 1,000. They contribute a huge amount as well. Sometimes they will send me something wonderful that they have bought in a period clothing shop and urge me to copy it or use it as my inspiration. My velvet outfits – particularly a crushed velvet smoking jacket – are big hits. Benazir Bhutto has one of my wraps, made in Pakistani national green, and another went to the daughter of the Georgian prime minister.

There has been no plain sailing. I think doing something like this means learning to cope with each emergency as it arrives. It means horrendous sleepless nights and God knows what.

It's not opting out, it's actually opting in. The other life was an easy life. If I was ill then somebody else would manage to cope with the work. If I am ill now nothing happens. It's utterly different.

Before I was living on the edge of life. Now I am actually trying to make it and create things for other people and really stick my oar in. It's made me much more independent and reasonably fearless – I'm sure it does that for everybody.

Peter Mantle was recuperating from his collapse by taking a fishing holiday in Ireland, when he discovered exactly how he would downshift. He spotted the derelict Delphi fishery in Galway and fell in love with it. There was no careful planning for him. Within two months he had quit his £60,000 a year job and bought the estate from the Marquis of Sligo for just over £200,000.

It was an overnight whim. Self-indulgent and crazy. My girlfriend, Jane, thought I had gone off my rocker, and my father was so cross he wouldn't speak to me for a week. It profoundly pissed him off.

I hadn't actually planned to abandon my career but the fishery took my breath away, even though it was derelict and would need millions spent on it.

The timing was right, job-wise. I loved what I was doing but regularly worked 100 hours a week. It was a treadmill – a very stimulating treadmill – but an unhealthy, knackering one. Without realising it, I was in severe danger of blowing all my head gaskets.

When I fell in love with Delphi, everything happened quickly. If it'd been thought out, we probably wouldn't have done it, because it was naive, short-sighted and dumb. Having quit I'd got no income apart from a bit of freelance work as a financial journalist to pay the mortgage, I was pretty broke and even went on the dole at one stage.

It took eight years to get the business on its feet, but now holiday-makers – including the Prince of Wales – come from Britain, the US and many other parts of the world to hunt and fish on Peter's 1,000 acres and stay in his rambling, 14-bedroom Victorian mansion. He employs 26 people and has married Jane; they have two children.

Lisa Nelson set up her company, PR Unlimited, at the age of 23. It quickly became one of the most successful fashion PR firms, working for The Gap, Laura Ashley and *The Clothes Show*. Lisa worked with 18 staff from a beautiful Georgian house in Westminster, she ran homes in London and Hampshire, had founded her own children's charity and had a happy marriage.

The ultimate handbook

If any woman had it all, it seemed, Lisa Nelson did.

Which made it all the more surprising when, out of the blue in September 1995, Lisa read the following statement to her staff:

I am no longer motivated by financial rewards or a budding ego. I want peace of mind and quality of life first and foremost. I have for a long time stated that I wish to have my own children and to work with disadvantaged inner-city children, and hoped to combine that with my business commitments.

That has not been possible. I started the Honeypot Home charity three years ago with this in mind, and actively started working with some children this summer. This is honestly where my heart lies and something I must explore further.

Lisa broke away to build a holiday home for underprivileged children, and it was the five inner-city children who stayed with her and her husband Richard at their rectory on the Hampshire – Wiltshire border who convinced her the plan would work.

Lisa's new working arrangements rely heavily on her supportive husband, who runs a small advertising and design company, and she has kept her hand in at her old profession, working as a freelance marketing consultant for an average of two days a week. Her charity has funds of £120,000, a full-time administrator and an office in the basement of her London home.

There are thousands of children who need that sort of thing.

I began to think that if there was a choice between earning lots of money and having a family, the family would be more important to me.

It's silly, really. You feel you can live a totally superficial life governed by money and material things and everything's fine. I actually felt embarrassed to say that I wanted to do something with children – and have some myself. Not that I have to prove anything now. I've proved I can run a business and be a reasonably good wife. Now is the time to do the things I really want to do.

And what I have done has struck a chord with many working women. I have had dozens of supportive letters. They said I had made them look at the superficiality of the world we live in, and the issue of women trying to do it all. I think that women can do it all, but at a cost. I'm sure that some people think I'm horrendous and mad ... my competitors, for instance, who are running around like headless chickens trying to get my clients.

In my naiveté, I thought it would be easy, but I know I'm viewed as a blonde ex-PR woman do-gooding; a rich spoilt housewife who wants to change the world. I know you can't change children's lives by giving them a holiday, but you can show them something different. A holiday can give them hope.

But there have been major problems to contend with. Just at the time Lisa was trying to convince local authorities of the benefits of a holiday service for deprived children, the trustee of another organisation, the Children's Country Holiday Fund, was accused of 'inappropriate touching' by a child. All holidays were suspended.

I was trying to persuade local authorities to let me provide holidays at the time. They all turned me down, but I would not take no for an answer and went from one office and authority to another until I found someone who agreed they had children who needed a break.

I was told not to cuddle the children, which is hard when they need it so badly. Nor may an adult be alone in a room with a child – difficult if one of them needs to talk confidentially or wants help going to the loo.

Dealing with disturbed children has not fazed me. At home, they have no toys and they sleep on the floor or three to a single bed. Many will have only one meal a day; here, they can't stop eating. If they have a tantrum it is not because they are spoilt, like some of my friends' children, but because they have a lot to deal with. Most of them are desperate to please. Some are bullies at school but they are sensitive inside, and it is their way of getting attention.

I am tough with them. I make them clear up. I tell them when to go to bed. They respond to discipline and feel safe within it.

To launch Honey Pot I sold my Mercedes, moth-balled my designer suits and gave up going out to dinner. To my amazement I haven't missed that life for a minute.

When Tim King decided to downshift he had no idea what he would do with his life.

Work was a treadmill, but I came alive at week-ends, hammering up the M11 to go hill-climbing or sail-ing. So I considered changing things in a small way, by moving from London chambers to the country. But then I thought 'No, if I'm going to change, go the whole hog.'

Then I found myself reminiscing about a holiday I had had in the Canadian Rockies. I remembered tramp-ing through the snow, and when I saw people actually working there I thought 'lucky bastards!' Those lumber-jacks had a physically satisfying job in a stunning place, so you could stick your feet up at the end of the day and feel contented.

So I went into a careers office in London and asked what leaflets they'd got on forestry. When I read them I thought, 'Yeah, this is me!'

Tim quit, and began studying for an HND in forestry. Itching to get his hands dirty, he went through the Yellow Pages, applying to every forestry company he could find for a job. He got one, lopping conifers, though it meant taking a cut in his weekly take-home pay from £500 to £160.

Now, having qualified, he plans to move to a Hebridean island and is busy looking for a job. He thinks everyone who feels the urge to downshift should follow their instincts.

The excuse people always use is, 'I'd love to, but I can't. I'll stay another year to save more money.' But that's just putting it off. People should grab the bull by the horns. If you've got those feelings, deal with them, because they don't go away. And all you end up with, if you ignore them, is regrets.

Even if you do not intend to downshift for the foreseeable future, it's a good idea to have a game plan laid out just in case. The fragile nature of the employment market means that having a structured downshifting plan tucked away is rather like holding an insurance policy – it's reassuring to know that it's there even if you never need to use it.

I was certainly glad that my plans were in place when I was fired out of the blue by the newspaper I had worked for four years. For the previous two years I had been preparing for what had just happened to me. It was a couple of years ago that, my wife Elena and I awoke with a nasty jolt to the fact that we needed to restructure our working lives in order to preserve the health of our family.

I remember vividly how it came about. It was the morning of my son Freddie's fifth birthday. I awoke alone. Elena had been working for all but two hours of the previous night. She had managed to return home briefly in the early hours from her job as producer of a live discussion programme on daytime TV, to grab a shower and change of clothes and to make sure I had not forgotten Freddie's birthday. I was to give Freddie his presents before I left the house at 8 a.m., and to leave the *au pair* with £20 and instructions to buy him a birthday cake.

I tried to bring some birthday fun to the morning in the few minutes I could spare, but I could see that Freddie was unhappy. That night, Elena told me he had said to her, 'Mummy, is it really my birthday?'

What had made him wonder was the simple fact that neither of us was around sufficiently to make him feel that the day was in any way special.

It was a sobering time for both of us. We realised then that we had to re-order our lives if they were to be worth living or, more importantly, if our children were to have a happy, secure and fulfilled childhood.

From that moment we started to plan.

The immediate requirement was that at least one of us had to work shorter hours. The main obstacle, however, was our massive mortgage.

We considered, and quickly rejected, the idea of moving to a cheaper home. This was our dream house and we were not going to give it up. That meant that our goal, and the key to downshifting for real, was to halve our mortgage repayments by paying back a substantial part of the loan.

We both felt it best that I be the one to resign from my job and instead work from home as a freelance writer and editor, with Elena the main breadwinner. We planned to live on Elena's salary and bank everything I could make; we

I Have a Dream...

thought that in this way we could save up enough to reach our goal in about two to three years' time. At that point, we reasoned, we would both be free to work part-time, ideally from home.

Then, to my surprise, when I told my employers I needed to quit I was offered promotion and a substantial pay rise to stay.

This changed the equation completely. If I were to accept the promotion and increase in pay, we could more or less wipe out our mortgage totally in two years. But if I stayed at work, Elena would have to give up a job that she loved. We were completely torn. In the end we asked the children – a cop-out, perhaps, but we decided we needed their input. Without a hint of hesitation, they stated that Elena should be the one who worked from home and be around for them more.

That settled it. I accepted the new position and Elena resigned hers. With great luck, she managed to find less demanding work with a new employer whose enlightened attitude meant that she could work flexible hours and take all the children's holidays off. In return, she worked extremely hard for short bursts when she was really needed.

In order to open up for ourselves the option of a really major downshift in the future, we did have to cut back drastically on our expenditure, suspending our plans to carry out major and expensive work on the house, and save furiously. We found that by tightening our belts we could save everything that Elena earned.

Meanwhile, I was able to plan exactly what I would do with my time if and when my 'Downshifting Day' eventually arrived. I cultivated the contacts which I knew I'd need if I were to freelance successfully, and planned what I would do with the rest of my time. I had two interests I wanted to develop: horticulture and the Italian language.

I am a keen amateur gardener, and discovered from my local college that, by following a one-year course that would take up one afternoon and one evening each week, I could gain a basic qualification in horticulture and another in garden design. That would open up two possibilities – the chance of work with a local garden design business and the option of writing about gardening – both of which could provide alternative sources of income.

My interest in Italian stems from the fact that Elena is from Italy. Family connections opened up the possibility of spending our summers there, should we both be freed from the constraints of full-time employment.

Two years on and, mercifully, I was ready to put this plan into practice when I got the push.

I am confident that many could benefit from having a plan for downshifting worked out in their heads.

DECISIONS

Perhaps you are already convinced that downshifting is for you. Perhaps you know what you will do and how to go about it. Maybe you have already recognised yourself in one or more of the case studies above – if not, you will certainly find someone like you by the end of this book.

But, most likely, you view the thought of downshifting with some trepidation. You are not sure if it is for you or if you are cut out for it. So how do you decide?

Maybe you find it helps to get clear in your head what you want to do by thinking about the areas of life that down-shifting will affect, to decide whether you are happy with them or not, and to think objectively about how you would change them.

Below I have listed these areas and, beneath each heading, posed a series of pertinent questions. Ask yourself the questions. Use the ones that are most relevant to you to help you reach conclusions about your present circumstances and about downshifting as an option.

You can use answering the questions to prompt you to write down a series of statements about yourself. Each statement will be a conclusion you have reached about yourself and your present predicament. Such statements will provide a firm record of your thinking. They will be something you can look back over in a week, a month or a year and decide whether you still feel the same way. Perhaps by then you will feel you were merely going through a bad patch at work or in a relationship, and that things look much brighter now. Or maybe you will feel exactly the same. Either way, your written statements will help you to reach a balanced decision about whether or not to downshift. In subsequent chapters I will be asking more questions and inviting you to come to more conclusions about yourself – more detailed questions about, for instance, exactly what activities you plan to undertake, and how you will cope on a much reduced income.

By the end of this book you will have built up a detailed testimony about yourself, your dissatisfactions, your plans and how to put them into action. It will be the equivalent to presenting a business plan to a bank manager, a concrete statement of intent, a plan for your new life.

Work

Just how bad is it at work?

You may find it helps in quantifying your dissatisfaction to set yourself the following 10-statement test, which was devised by Dr Adrian Furnham, Psychology Professor at University College, London.

He believes that rapid change in work is causing burnout among many workers, and that the drive for leaner and meaner oganisations has increased emotional, physical and psychological exhaustion among staff.

Classic symptoms, he says, include an idea that work is meaningless, a hostility towards the employer's aims, and a sense of powerlessness.

The causes of burn-out include heavy work, boredom, poor communication and too much responsibility.

Here are his 10 statements:

1 I feel that my work drains me emotionally.
2 I seem to treat clients and colleagues like objects.
3 I feel too exhausted and fatigued at the beginning of the day.
4 I have definitely become more callous and devious at work.
5 I feel I am working harder than others at work.
6 I think the job is hardening me emotionally.
7 Working with people (clients, colleagues) is a real strain.
8 I don't care what happens to the firm or the staff.
9 I feel pretty much at the end of my tether.
10 I believe my colleagues blame me for their problems.

Determine your score based on your chosen response to each statement:

Never	1
Once or twice	2
About once a week	3
A few times a week	4
Every day	5

If your score is 40 or above you are at – or near – burn-out.

You might also like to consider the following, more

I Have a Dream...

general questions about work and your feelings towards it, which I have compiled after talking to many downshifters:

▼ Have you achieved your ambitions in work?
▼ Have you decided your ambitions are no longer worthy of you?
▼ Have you decided your ambitions will never be achieved?
▼ Is your job secure?
▼ Can you see yourself doing well in 10 years' time?
▼ When you look at those in your company or profession who are 10 years older than you, would you be happy to end up like them?
▼ How important to your self-image is the position you hold at work?

Health

▼ How is your health?
▼ Are work and the stresses of work affecting it?
▼ Do you exercise?
▼ How vulnerable are you to serious illness? Is there a history of heart disease in your family, perhaps?
▼ Do you drink too much, smoke too much or take drugs because of the pressures of work?

Relationships

▼ Do you have a partner?
▼ Is your lifestyle getting in the way of forming or sustaining personal relationships?
▼ If you are married or in a stable relationship, how healthy is it?
▼ Is your career getting in the way of your starting a family or, if you have children, damaging your relationship with them?

The ultimate handbook

Lifestyle

▼ Do you spend freely, keeping your credit cards at their absolute limit?

▼ Are you a conspicuous consumer or a conserver?

▼ How important is it to you to have the best of everything?

▼ How strongly do you feel the need to drive a new car, have a large wardrobe and take expensive holidays?

Other Interests

▼ Does work leave you time for other interests – from sports and hobbies to charity work?

▼ Would you like to widen your range of interests and commitments?

▼ Do you feel the need to do something useful, something that will help others rather than benefit you?

Overview

▼ Do you feel that you are fulfilled as a person?

▼ Are you in general an asset to the world? If not, do you want to be?

CHAPTER TWO

Do You Seriously Want to Be Poor?

OF COURSE, you might not end up poor at all. Paradoxically, downshifting does make a few people rich. But the best that you can realistically hope for is that you will end up poorer financially but richer in contentment and in happiness.

It has to be faced, though, that for some, attempting to downshift becomes an unmitigated disaster.

Mark Caines left accountancy to invent board games and make his fortune. Three years later he was an accountant again, and still paying off his debts. He describes his years of downshifting as a total failure.

Tony Blackler gave up his job as a chartered accountant to move with his wife to become the 'lord' of the island of Lundy. His job was to bring calm to the tiny community on this speck of land in the Bristol Channel after his predecessor left when his marriage broke up. Tony resigned after seven months. He and his wife, Cherry, had failed to anticipate the ravages of the Atlantic in winter.

Cherry said: 'Tony would go off the mainland for a meeting and then get stranded because of the weather. It reached the point when we never saw each other, and that seemed to defeat the whole purpose of going to Lundy in the first place.'

Jane and Stephen Simmonds moved with their two young children to a village in the countryside. But they hated village life after living in inner London and now want to go back to the city again.

So. It is probably time for a Health Warning: Downshifting can seriously damage your wealth, and set you on a road that you find you really do not want to follow.

In a nutshell, if fear of failure or of making a major mistake is a serious concern, you are probably better off forgetting the whole idea of downshifting before it is too late.

If downshifting sounds as reckless as bungee-jumping, if you class risking your financial security with leaping off the Clifton Suspension Bridge attached to a length of elastic, if downshifting sounds like an extremely risky act that might be exciting but could very easily end in disaster – don't do it.

Of course, the bungee-jump analogy is one legitimate way of looking at downshifting. In a sense you will be leaping off the high ledge of gainful employment, and into the abyss.

It is not difficult to imagine your friends and colleagues watching you plummet earthwards, all wondering with some interest whether the rubber will snap. And, if it does hold and twang you back up again before your head hits the ground, where will you end up? Will you be deposited safely on one of the lower financial ledges that you are aiming for, or will you merely be pinged up and down in ever decreasing arcs until the motion eventually ceases, leaving you dangling helplessly in mid-air?

Fortunately, the bungee-jumping analogy is not the only one that can be applied to downshifting. There is another, far more reassuring one that can be drawn.

The management guru Charles Handy, in his book *The Empty Raincoat*, comes up with a wonderful model for life which I believe can be borrowed very effectively for the downshifter. He calls it the sigmoid curve.

Handy's sigmoid curve is in the shape of an S on its side, or perhaps a section of a rollercoaster ride where the track first dips so the train gains momentum, then climbs doggedly up to a peak, before whizzing off down the other side.

Handy uses it to represent the average pattern of life, and of a career. We start slowly and falteringly, dropping into the first trough, he says, before we begin to rise, reaching our peak somewhere in middle age before declining into old age.

Downshifters are seeking to deviate from that curve before decline sets in, before they are doomed to live out the rest of their lives in the same old rut. In Handy's terms, they are seeking to create a new sigmoid curve for themselves, a curve which lifts off from the old curve at some point before it begins its final descent, or before that descent gets too severe.

That new curve lifts the downshifter up on a new rising curve, a new arc that sweeps him or her upwards into a new life.

With such a model, the downshifter is not plunging down. Instead he is performing a gentle take-off manoeuvre, then rising as – to use a third analogy – a hang-glider pilot would who has read the upcurrents correctly when he leaps off a cliff.

It could all go wrong, of course. The new curve may prove actually to be a vertiginous plunge into failure and poverty – the bungee-jump gone wrong, in which the elastic snaps and the downshifter is doomed.

Which will it be? Success or failure? That is the challenge a downshifter faces.

It is the question posed for every downshifter as he or she makes the leap into the unknown. Ultimately, it has to be

Do You Seriously Want to Be Poor?

admitted, no individual can know the answer until he or she has made the leap – or whatever you want to call it – and experienced what happens. But there are many things that can be done in advance to ensure that all precautions have been taken.

IS DOWNSHIFTING FOR ME?

The most fundamental, of course, is to decide whether you personally are cut out for downshifting. Can you cope with the risks? Will you thrive away from the aggressive, competitive world of conventional employment, or will the loss of your high-powered job leave a huge hole in your life? Are you cut out for this new, more uncertain world? Have you a clear idea of what you will do? Can you cope on what could be a drastically reduced income? Will you be happy downshifting, or would you be much better off if you admitted that it is not for you and abandoned it as a rash daydream before it is too late?

This chapter is designed to help unsuitable candidates disqualify themselves from downshifting before they do anything rash or drastic.

One area to be very sure about is that of work. Men in particular need to face the fact that the ethic of work is deeply ingrained in their psyche. Although hardly any of them would admit it, many men see themselves as the brave hunter, going out every day into the steamy corporate jungle, off to kill or be killed, and to bring back meat to the little woman who has spent the day keeping the cave tidy and nurturing the young.

Anyone in a career, man or woman, needs to acknowledge the fact that a demanding, important job gives them their status in the world and a sense of purpose. Work defines us. It is an important building block in the image others have

The ultimate handbook

of us – and of our self-image. Take it away and there is a risk that you will lose a sense of purpose and of identity.

Men and women in the professional classes were raised to labour, to honour sweat and revere the profit motive. It is hard for skilled, educated and experienced people to adapt to a new life.

Some experts say giving up a fast-track career can be as emotionally wrenching and physically demanding as withdrawal from an addiction.

What Do I Want?

The second big question every downshifter must ask is: What is the minimum lifestyle I am prepared to accept?

The equation of what your new income will be is a complex one, because it depends on all sorts of other very important things such as what work you decide to do, how much voluntary work you wish to undertake, where you decide to live, and so on. For now, all you can do is to rough out a fairly simple sum.

First, work out what your expenditure is each month. To ensure that you include occasional items, go through your accounts for a minimum of the past three months. Then work out how much less you could manage on. You will need to decide what you are prepared to cut out. There is no hard-and-fast formula for what constitutes a downshifted income and what does not. It is entirely up to you. For you, downshifting may mean surviving with one car and having a five-bedroom house instead of an eight-bedroom one or, at the other extreme, it may mean living in a remote, two-room croft without electricity or running water and surviving by bartering with your neighbours.

The choice, as they tell contestants on *Blind Date*, is yours. But here are a few questions which will be relevant to most downshifters.

▼ Can you reduce your mortgage by using your savings?
▼ If you have other debts on a car or other items, can you pay them off?
▼ Do you need to sell your house to get a smaller mortgage?
▼ Should you sell the car and get a cheaper one?
▼ If you have enjoyed taking expensive holidays, will you have to give them up?
▼ If you have children in fee-paying schools, are you prepared to move them into the state system? What would they feel about that?

Before you proceed, it is important to have a figure in mind of the minimum income you could live on. At this stage in your progress towards deciding if downshifting is for you, and how it is going to work in your own case, this can only be a preliminary figure, but it is a start, and something to be kept very much in mind as you go through this book and reach all kinds of important decisions on what you will do and where you will live.

With a clear idea of what level of affluence you want, what you are prepared to do without and an idea of the minimum you are prepared to live on, you will be able to begin to focus on the possible things you might do in your new life.

Some people are prepared to make drastic economies, others are not. Some will give up all the trappings of success, others are determined to keep some of them.

The ultimate handbook

Will I Last the Course?

Let us look in more detail at the other big question: Are you cut out to downshift?

From speaking to over 50 downshifters, most of whom have succeeded in their task, some of whom have failed, I have come up with a checklist of the qualities that successful downshifters tend to have in common. Successful downshifters tend to be:

- ▼ independent and self-reliant
- ▼ brave, confident, optimistic, resilient and enterprising
- ▼ full of energy and enthusiasm
- ▼ keener to conserve than to consume
- ▼ blessed with a sense of humour
- ▼ not reliant on the approval of others for their self-esteem
- ▼ willing to try again should they fail
- ▼ honest and reliable
- ▼ risk-takers when they believe in something, and able to cope with the unexpected
- ▼ prepared to make sacrifices
- ▼ questioning of the status quo
- ▼ able to take the initiative, coming quickly to decisions
- ▼ optimistic and tenacious
- ▼ able to take criticism when it is warranted
- ▼ good listeners and keen to learn from others
- ▼ able to prioritise in order to spend time on the things they enjoy the most
- ▼ highly organised
- ▼ patient
- ▼ hard-working and able to enjoy problem-solving
- ▼ aware of their strengths and weaknesses
- ▼ creative and imaginative.

It cannot be stressed too strongly that successful downshifting depends on defining exactly what you want from life. Downshifters must act decisively rather than procrastinating. They need to be able to define exactly what they need to do to achieve their goals – what skills they must learn, what sacrifices they must make, what changes they must adapt to – and to get on with it. They need to be adept at confronting problems and obstacles to progress and solving them, rather than ignoring them and allowing them to blight progress. They also, however, have to know when a problem is insurmountable and when to give up on something, or live with an unchangeable reality.

Essentially, downshifting is about choice. It is about choosing exactly what you want to do. Many who downshift have great abilities, aptitudes, strengths and skills and have decided that, if they downshift successfully, these skills can be put to better or more rewarding use, or to aid the social good.

Here are some indicators that you might *not* be suited to downshifting:

▼ You enjoy the security of having an organisation around you.
▼ You enjoy office politics and the camaraderie of office life. You enjoy the company of your colleagues so much that you regularly spend time socialising with them after work rather than going home.
▼ You tend to work long hours out of habit rather than because it is strictly necessary.
▼ Your job gives you a status that you feel it would be hard to replace.
▼ You gain a sense of your own self-worth from the things your job buys you – your house, car and general lifestyle.

- ▼ The struggles and successes of your professional life are more real to you – or more enjoyable – than those in your private life.
- ▼ You feel that a sideways or downward move would end your career.
- ▼ You want more money.
- ▼ You cannot relax.
- ▼ Domestic life seems full of chores rather than pleasures.
- ▼ You gain your sense of confidence from security rather than tackling the unknown.
- ▼ You are afraid of the unknown sacrifices you might have to make.
- ▼ You fear a drop in income.
- ▼ You are heavily in debt, a victim of negative equity or you have insufficient savings or equity in your home.
- ▼ You have no idea what you could earn if you down-shifted, or what you might do with your time.
- ▼ Your excuses for not having downshifted so far are because you will wait until your career suffers a set-back – either you are fired, made redundant or are seriously blocked for promotion.
- ▼ You want to see someone else downshift before you will try it.

Let us look in detail at three people I introduced at the start of this chapter whose attempts to downshift left them dissatisfied:

Mark Caines failed because his business plan did not work. He was an accountant in Bristol when, at the age of 26, he decided to give up his job and produce and market the board games he invented. Three years later he was an accountant again. The business failed, and so did his marriage.

When I look back it is as if I was a different person then, as if I am looking at what a stranger has done with their lives. My plan was to get out once and for all, to never have to return to the rat race and never work again in my life, but it didn't work out. When I look back it is over three years of stress and worry – of nothing really. Nothing achieved and nothing won.

I broke out because I had just had it with accountancy. One day I just couldn't stay in the office any longer, I just had to get out so I went for a walk to clear my head. That happened a few times. I'd be looking at a list of figures and I just couldn't take them in any more.

Ever since I was a teenager I had been fascinated by board games. One day I was at a property auction and I got the idea for a board game about the property business. That was it, I would leave work and invent and market the game.

My wife couldn't understand what was wrong with me. She came from an accountancy background and she didn't understand why I wanted to rebel against it. She couldn't understand the drive I felt, and she thought I was mad to be giving it up.

Then I got an offer from a client, who asked if I wanted to become a director of his construction company. I went away to Morocco to think about it. My family said I should take it, that I would have the freedom that I wanted, but would also be safe. They thought the game was a hopeless risk. But I was determined to stick with it, even if it was the biggest gamble of my life.

It spelled the end of the marriage and we divorced.

First of all I worked part-time, 15 hours a week, and was only earning £5,000 instead of £14,000. I sold my house, which was a very nice four-bedroom place

The ultimate handbook

and which gave me £7,000 to invest in the game, which I called Prosperity, *and I swapped my Cavalier for a Polo. I put my furniture in storage and moved into a £10-a-week bedsit.*

I invested £20,000 in the game, but although my ideas were good I was naive. I got carried away with my own enthusiasm. Trying to get the games in the shops – I also developed one based on the Mafia called Mob – proved more frustrating than I'd ever envisaged. I rang one of the biggest toy shops 20 times in a week and didn't even get a reply. It felt like I'd swapped one hamster wheel for another.

In the end I had to admit defeat. My biggest mistake was to employ a consultant at £400 a month who told me he could get the games marketed. He couldn't.

I was so short of cash that I moved in with my sister and took a part-time accountancy job.

I finally admitted defeat and started my own freelance accountancy firm. Now I have 90 clients and an annual turnover of £60,000, but I am still paying off the last of the debts I built up in the three years I was trying to market my games.

The most valuable lesson it taught me is to be pragmatic and realistic, because when the heart rules the head it brings disaster. There are a lot of creative people in suits out there, but I'd advise them to look at alternatives within their working framework before going off in a completely different direction.

Tony and Cherry Blackler went to Lundy, a former pirates' lair 18 miles off the North Devon coast, in order to spend more time together. Tony, who is an accountant and also breeds cattle and runs a nature reserve on a 12-acre plot in Cornwall, was appointed agent for the Landmark Trust, which runs the island. They gave up their farmhouse, complete with indoor heated swimming pool, for a modern flat in a staff block at the foot of a wind-lashed hill. In fact, the rigours of life there put their marriage under strain, and they had to admit defeat. Cherry says:

When we got the job we put our smallholding in Cornwall up as a holiday let. We thought we would never need it, but Tony was stuck on the mainland so much that we had to take it off the rental list just so that he could have a base, somewhere to have a bath and hang his clothes.

Even when the sea was relatively calm, the boat sailed only once a week or so in winter. Tony used to have to cadge a lift with the helicopter rescue crew at RAF Chivenor, near Barnstaple, on the mainland. There are only so many times you can call in those kind of favours. As a result we'd be apart for days at a time, and that seemed to defeat the whole purpose of us going to Lundy in the first place. We might as well have been leading separate lives.

Tony was responsible for overall management of the island's livestock, marine nature reserve, historic monuments – including a 13th-century castle and a smugglers' cave – holiday properties, food and fuel stores, shop, pub and an electricity generator and well:

In many ways our seven months on the island were absolutely horrendous.

The final straw came when we returned from a wonderful holiday in India. I had a meeting with the Landmark Trust but Cherry went straight back to Lundy. By the time I'd finished on the mainland the weather made it impossible to reach her. We were apart for another 10 days and that was just one time too many.

It may have been an isolated life at times, but it was never quiet. That was as we expected, with 20,000 visitors a year. Hard work is something we enjoy and it certainly wasn't the reason for leaving. I don't regret taking the job. It has been a fascinating, and often hilarious experience, and we still love Lundy very much. We will go back to visit. At the moment we just want to stay at home, walk the labradors, maybe watch a few badgers or otters and slowly ease our way back into work. Most of all, we just want to be together.

Jane and Stephen Simmonds moved from Notting Hill, West London, to the Sussex countryside to give their children a better quality of life. Jane tells their story:

I thought living in the countryside would be like London, only greener. It never occurred to me that people would be so different. It was like stepping back into the 1950s. Life was so conventional. The women in the village expected me to make jam and cakes for their stalls and hold coffee mornings. I felt I was being shoehorned into the role of a sweet, homely housewife, and I hated it.

I didn't feel like that at first. Initially, we loved it. The schools were so much better, the children could play in the fields and woods in safety and they quickly settled in and found new friends.

But the peace and quiet did not compensate for what we were missing in London. Life is so much richer there, and I felt that as the children got towards their teens, I wanted them to experience it, and not be stuck in the narrow existence we have down here. I wanted them to have wide horizons, to feel that they could do anything they wished, and village life just encourages people to settle for what is on their doorstep.

Also, the secondary schools are not as good as the primary ones, and it is a 30-mile round trip to take them to a cinema or a swimming pool. It is frustrating for me as well. I have stuck it for five years, but I want to get a job again now, and there is nothing here apart from packing chickens in the local slaughterhouse. As soon as we can, we will move back to London.

DECISIONS

Chapter 1 was all about gauging your level of dissatisfaction with your lot. Chapter 2 has been about deciding whether downshifting could present a relevant solution to your problems.

Now it is time to try to decide whether you are cut out for downshifting. The lists above of qualities that successful downshifters tend to share – and those that failed downshifters have in common – should help you to see which camp you belong in. Below I have tried to crystallise those long lists into a few essential areas for consideration, and a number of questions to answer about yourself.

Think about the areas, answer the questions and come up with a series of statements about yourself to add to those you made after reading Chapter 1.

The Lure of a High-powered Career

▼ Are you afraid of turning your back on a high-powered career?
▼ Do you worry that you might be jeopardising your career if you step out of it now?
▼ Could you replace it with other things which are more fulfilling?

▼ Can you make work less important to you than your family, friends, home life, hobbies and other interests?

If you are unsure of exactly how you feel about your job, keep a log. Put a circle in your diary around every day that you say 'I must leave.' If, flicking through your diary, there are more circles than unmarked days, it's time to go.

What Are Your Priorities?

▼ Are you cut out to take a major risk in your life? Do you enjoy taking risks and chances, or do you loathe doing so?
▼ How materialistic are you?
▼ Would you suffer a loss of your sense of self-worth and identity if you could not have fashionable clothes, a smart car, expensive foreign holidays and a generally affluent lifestyle?
▼ How practical, resourceful and self-reliant are you?
▼ Do you have a clear idea of what you want to do?
▼ Do you make constant excuses for not getting out?

If any of these apply to you, downshifting may not be the right choice. You may prefer to leave it as a comforting dream, as something you will consider seriously if things get really bad, but not before.

CHAPTER THREE

Hello, I'm Your Mummy and This Is Your Daddy

A LITTLE while ago a controversial book was published in the US which argued the case that the film industry was, because of the 'warped values' presented in the movies, helping to destroy the country. It was called *Hollywood versus America*.

I see a more fundamental and insidious threat to modern society. If I were to write a book about it I would entitle it *Work versus the Family*.

Career has gained an over-riding importance in the lives of many professional people – both men and women – to the detriment of their relationships with each other and with their children.

For very many of those downshifters who have children, the desire for a better family life and the determination to be better parents than they would otherwise have the time and energy to be are the central spurs behind their decision to downshift.

Sue White almost lost her first son during a very difficult birth. She and her husband Colin decided that all their priorities were wrong. They both gave up full-time work to be with the baby, reasoning that as he was the most important thing in their lives he deserved as much of their time as they could give him.

Solicitors Tim and Dierdre Powell found a job they could share in order that they could split the child-care equally.

Di Reed left Bradford and her high-powered job in advertising so that she and husband Colin could realise their dream of living in their favourite holiday spot. They did so because they were convinced it was the perfect place in which to bring up children.

For such people, and many thousands more, the decision to downshift has come about as a result of their conviction that for both partners in a relationship to work full-time at demanding, high-pressure jobs is to leave far too little time for those who matter most – their children.

This is something of a sea change. For the conventional wisdom during the 1980s was that it was perfectly possible to juggle a job and family commitments – to have it all.

Since then, things have changed. For women there has been a recognition that the eighties belief in juggling several roles – career woman, wife, mother, home-maker, lover, friend – was a misguided one. The idea that you could deal with your family commitments in short, intensified bursts of what was called 'quality time' has been exposed for what it always was – a myth.

For men, who all along remained more focused on their careers to the exclusion of partner and family, there has come bitterness and resentment. While men were doing what they believed they had to do – focusing on being a good bread-winner – their children were growing up without them, and their marriages were atrophying.

The ultimate handbook

Parents At Work, a pressure group that campaigns to make companies more family-friendly, confirmed in a report published in November 1995 that:

...72 per cent of working mothers report always being exhausted at the end of the day; one in five say their marriages are at risk: and three out of five mothers say they don't see enough of their children.

Workplace pressure means mothers often rush home from work to spend some time with their children – only to work late into the evening when the children are asleep.

And they are too afraid of losing their jobs, the report goes on, to work shorter hours. The report concludes: 'Our research confirms that Britain's long-hours culture is seriously undermining the quality of life. We must challenge this culture, for everyone's sake.'

High divorce rates are also blamed by many on career pressures. In Surrey, for example, where divorce rates are the highest in Europe (at 40 per cent), the Mothers' Union blames demanding jobs and the pressure of commuting for the sobering statistic.

Anne Fraser, president of the Guildford diocese Mothers' Union, said at a conference called The Stopping Train Through Divorce and Beyond, 'Even those couples in good jobs are finding it increasingly difficult to stay together as the demands of work and the long hours involved in high-powered posts take their toll on marriages.'

Sharon Pilkington, co-organiser of the conference, said constant pressure to succeed also played a very important part. 'In the south east especially there is a great deal of pressure to always achieve and to go up the next rung of the ladder. This can put massive strain on any marriage.'

Hello, I'm Your Mummy and This Is Your Daddy

Simon Sperryn, chief executive of the London Chamber of Commerce, believes that the recognition of this dangerous situation – and the desire to do something about it by changing working arrangements – could become so widespread that, as he suggested in a seminar for the Working Parents Employer of the Year awards, there is a new class of family emerging, with both parents working part-time and bringing up the children together.

It is not difficult to find people who share this view.

Professor Cary Cooper of the University of Manchester Institute of Science and Technology (UMIST) is the leading authority on stress. He recognises that the stress of working too hard was a possible factor in the break up of his first marriage. Now in *Who's Who*, he places 'enjoying my four children' high on his list of recreations, but he realises that the reality for many is that they must spend less time at home if they are to keep their jobs.

'Most organisations are cutting down,' he said in an interview in *The Times* with Valerie Grove. 'So ... people are doing more work and working longer hours out of insecurity ... staying longer at work because they don't want to be included in the next tranche of redundancies ... they get home later and then have conflicts over who should be doing what.'

So how can we achieve a healthy balance between home and work?

More and more parents have come to recognise that dual full-time careers can harm relationships and family life, and that quality time can easily turn into opulent neglect – the affliction suffered by children of working parents whose mothers and fathers lavish material rewards on them but are too busy to give them the attention they need, whenever they need it.

I am well aware that this is an argument which will go down very well with traditionalists who believe that a woman's place is in the home and that many modern ills can be placed at the feet of women who forsake this habitat for the 'man's world' of work. But I don't intend for one minute to suggest that returning women to the home as full-time housewives is the solution, any more than it would be for men to stay permanently at home while their partners worked. Neither men nor women will benefit if one of them is given sole responsibility for earning the income, and the other the exclusive duty of child-rearing.

The authoritative Social Trends survey says the average British father works 53 hours a week. If he is totally focused on work in this way, a man can have little time or energy left for family life. To someone working such hours, children are strangers who grunt at him in the kitchen at dawn. One question a father who is considering the merits of downshifting might profitably ask himself is 'How many minutes do I spend talking to the children each week?'

Of course, the traditionalist might see nothing much wrong in all this. Certainly, a generation ago many people would have said that a man's role in family life was that of feared judge and executioner, the ultimate deterrent when mother's rule was being flouted.

This is no longer good enough for many fathers – and certainly not good enough for those who have decided to downshift. Today, we want to establish a rapport with our sons and daughters based on love rather than fear. We would like to think that we are around enough to be able to pass on a code for them to live decently and happily, that we can give them moral and ethical guidelines, rather than the odd clip round the ear.

Both men and women have been living untenable lives. One sex should not blame the other. Rather, we should all recognise the solution: downshifting. Downshifting gives the balance that is missing in other, less equitable arrangements

Hello, I'm Your Mummy and This Is Your Daddy

of work and family responsibilities. It embodies the concept of sharing, as the individuals in the case studies have done in their various ways.

Colin White cut his working week from five to three days. He is a management development specialist for British Telecom. He and his wife Sue live in Holingden, a village 10 miles from Milton Keynes, with their sons Adam (8) and Matthew (5), and daughter Hannah (1).

We very nearly lost Adam. Sue haemorrhaged right at the end of what had up till then been a textbook pregnancy. The consultant said Adam should not have survived, so he is a bit of a miracle child.

Of course, every child is precious, but coming so close to losing him made Adam even more so. That was the driving force behind my deciding I wanted to work part-time. It made me focus on what is really important in life. I wanted to spend more time with him because we so very nearly lost him.

Up until then I had not exactly been career mad but my job was very important to me. But then I decided my family was more important.

So now Sue works on Mondays and Tuesdays as a teacher and I work Wednesday to Friday, so we always have one of us at home with the children.

As no one else had ever gone part-time in my office I thought it would be very difficult to arrange, but in fact it was straightforward. My boss was extremely supportive which, given that he has no children and is a workaholic, was very understanding of him.

Until recently BT as a company was busy encouraging people to go, but now they are valuing people more. I am firmly of the opinion that if you can meet your staff's needs then you are more likely to get the

The ultimate handbook

best out of them. If I had not got what I wanted I would either have left or, if that proved impossible, carried on but with a great deal of resentment towards the company. But the fact they were able to meet my needs means I am prepared to give a lot of effort to them.

We feel more secure with both of us having jobs. In the traditional set-up where the man is the provider and the woman stays home, it does put a lot of responsibility on the man, especially in times where work is very uncertain.

And I have spare time to do other things that interest me now that work is not squeezing everything else into the corner. I was a counsellor for Relate for five years, and I saw a lot of people whose marriages had come under strain, where the balance had gone wrong.

In the traditional set-up a man and woman can find it very difficult. You can get the man working very hard and the woman stuck at home. The man sits there thinking 'This is dreadful, I've got to go to work, isn't it awful at the office' and the woman feels trapped at home with the children. Each finds it difficult to see the other's point of view.

Now with my spare time I have become involved with the school which Adam and Matthew attend, which is just up the road. I know the teachers very well and pop into the school to help with classes. I go to the open assemblies and things like that, so I know what the boys are up to.

The village is very small and nothing ever happens here! If you are around like I am, even if am just pushing Hannah for a stroll in her pushchair, I meet people. It gives balance. We have a bungalow with a nice garden – we bought it for the garden long before we thought of having children.

Financially there have been sacrifices, but we are happy being poor! In fact we only go without the luxuries, never the essentials. We can't have a nice car or foreign holidays, and the ski boots have been in the loft for about 10 years, though I still have a longing look at them when I am up there.

I know that a lot of people would like to come to the sort of work arrangement that we have, but I am not sure that we are moving towards it as a society. An awful lot of people are having more and more demands placed on them at work. And yet there is a whole army of people out of work.

To my mind, if people in work are stressed and harassed and those out of it are feeling worthless you might as well cut things in half and share the available work – give everyone half a job.

Tim Powell has job-shared as a solicitor with his wife Deirdre in Tulse Hill, South London, for five years. The office has five solicitors in a total staff of 16. Tim works every Monday, Wednesday and Thursday, Deirdre works Tuesdays and Fridays. They have a full-time secretary who provides continuity between them, and they divide their workload as it suits them. They have two children, Katie (6) and Johnnie (3^1/$_2$).

Deirdre was very worried that once she had children she would be out of work for 10 or 15 years, but I decided that I wanted to have a part in their upbringing.

That was in 1989. Deirdre was on maternity leave and I wanted to leave the job I had with a firm of solicitors in the West End, so the obvious answer was for us to look for a job we could share. We would work two or three days a week each and share the child-care between us – not have a nanny or an au pair.

The ultimate handbook

Job-shares like ours are practically unknown, but Deirdre mentioned the idea to an acquaintance she met at court who was a partner in a firm of solicitors in Tulse Hill. He had a vacancy but he said at first that a job-share would not work. But there was a shortage of lawyers at the time and, as they had no other applicants, we were granted an interview. We were both very experienced and had such a range of skills to offer that we got the job.

We both work less and are under less stress and strain. I get to spend time at home during the week, which is something that, in the eighties, I had no experience of. It is very pleasant. I have spent five-and-a-half years bringing up my children, which I could not have done if I was working full-time. That has been an irreplaceable experience. I am much closer to my children than I would be otherwise, and I have a very strong relationship with them. I don't think it could have been as strong if I had not done this.

I go into school. I was there this morning. Each Tuesday I help out in Katie's class. I'm not qualified to teach so I just do whatever it is the teacher wants me to. So it could be one-to-one reading for a child that needs some help or floating around the class from group to group. Today we were doing addition so I was helping children use an abacus and count on their fingers.

So there is a tangible benefit in my working part-time for more than just me, my wife and my children.

We are not as well off, certainly, living on one salary. If we had two salaries and a nanny there is no doubt we would be miles better off. We would be wealthy, we could have foreign holidays and two cars and a bigger house. Lots of our friends both work full-time or

Hello, I'm Your Mummy and This Is Your Daddy

one full- and one part-time and they've all got more money than we have. So that is the trade-off.

We didn't sit down and do careful financial calculations. We just decided to live on one salary.

Usually people are surprised we are doing this and quite pleased to discover that it exists – quite amused and interested. There is some ... envy is a strong word but lots say they would like to do something similar, 'if only ...' We always try and encourage people to change their set-up even if it is only one day a week or an afternoon or anything. Because once you start to change the traditional set-up you realise that it is possible and you can develop it further as time goes by.

We have many friends who work long, long hours and they are completely devoted to their jobs. They love the office politics and they love the sphere of work. It is just no use babbling on to them about how nice it is pushing a buggy up a street on a Tuesday morning. But we are always very positive about it because it works so well for us.

Having been there and done it during the 1980s and having done it differently now I find it surprising that people are still wedded to the way of working that I gave up. But you have to face it that sometimes people are on a very definite career progression and they don't dare do anything that would upset it. And they are fearful of changing as we have.

Working part-time is a very liberating thing. Deirdre's fears of not working have not materialised. She has kept a proper job throughout.

I think our way of life is catching on. I have seen a change. I notice more and more men taking part in child-care. When I first started in 1990 I went to a toy library with Katie and I was the only man there. It was

The ultimate handbook

quite intimidating, but within three years there were on average three or four men there besides me. And there are more and more men bringing their children to school than there were even two or three years ago.

I get the feeling there is a rejigging of people's priorities. I know a lot of people who in recent times have gone down to four days a week or are on some sort of flexitime. I spoke to a civil servant recently and he basically crams his five days' work into four days through flexitime and takes every Friday off. His partner does the same and has Mondays free, so the children get more of their time.

Maybe things are more humane now, there seems to be more tolerance of those who want to work fewer hours for the sake of their family.

I would recommend it to anyone – just forgo a tenth of your salary and gain an amazing benefit.

Mike and Di Reed were able to realise their dream of moving to their favourite holiday spot on the shores of Loch Ouiron on Lewis because of modern technology. Di, a 39-year-old freelance advertising copywriter who is the main breadwinner, can do her job as well from there because of her computer as she could from an office in their former home of Bradford. Mike, 38, a self-employed maker of fishermen's flies, can work anywhere. The couple spent two Christmases on the island to see if they could put up with a place where the midwinter daylight lasts six hours and southwesterly gales howl in most days from the Atlantic.

They have three children – Harriet (4), Madeleine (3) and Alastair (1) – but also brought with them their two dogs, four cats and 22 carp.

Hello, I'm Your Mummy and This Is Your Daddy

Mike and I began to worry that the children were growing up behind our backs. I've got this old-fashioned idea that it's a parent's job to bring up children and that is not possible if you are out all day earning money.

Mike was working from home and raising the children and I was going to work, as I was the one who could earn more. I was the one who went off with a briefcase in the morning while he stayed at home and looked after the kids. We wanted another child – we had two when we moved – but decided that it was not possible with the lifestyle we were living at the time. So we took our skills and brought them with us to the island.

We then had Alastair, born in the Western Isles Hospital. He's 14 months old now, and gorgeous. In Bradford I was seeing the children at the weekends and for an hour before they went to bed. I was missing so much, missing them growing up.

We are still incredibly busy, both of us have got more work almost than we can cope with. I supply clients in Yorkshire and mainland Scotland and on the islands. Michael sells mail order and also supplies some tackle shops, but we can juggle work between us now that we are both at home, and make sure one of us is always there for the children. If we want to, we can work at 11 at night to get things done.

We are quite remote here. Stornaway, the capital, is 27 miles away, but the area suits our needs. There is a school here, a shop and a post office. It is also an extremely attractive location. There is masses of fishing within walking distance, which keeps Mike blissfully happy. We plan to offer fishing holidays here in the future.

To make a new life successfully, as we have done, you have to be very sure of what you are doing, and of

The ultimate handbook

exactly what you want. But the only way to find out is to do it.

It could have been a risk, but I turned up here and there are hardly any copywriters in the Highlands and Islands. We arrived with a way of making money. We brought our means of earning a living with us. I wouldn't like to turn up and then start looking for a job. The economics have to stack up. We took a risk, but we didn't have much to lose if it was a complete disaster. We had nothing in the first place. We broke even on our house sale and worked like hell to make a go of it here.

We suffered financially at first. I was five months' pregnant when we arrived and for the next six months I wasn't in a position to do much work. The first year was quite tough, we had to find money for the removal costs and for work that had to be done on the house.

I can't think of any other disadvantages. There is the weather, I suppose, but you can't expect it to be like Tenerife.

The children love it here. You can let them out without the risk of them being run over or meeting strange people. There is very little traffic and a very low crime rate.

If you came here with some romanticised view it could be very hard – but we didn't.

DECISIONS

If you are downshifting partly to improve the quality of your family life, you have to be sure that your family will appreciate what you are doing for them! Let's take the significant others one by one:

Your Partner

Is he or she with you? If not, forget it. You can do nothing unless you are united. Even a close, stable relationship can suffer when the protection of financial security suddenly disappears and one partner blames the other.

Children

What will your children's reaction be to leaving their schools and friends? How will they feel to lose pony rides, foreign holidays, trips to theme parks and clothing allowances? Can you convince them that there are other advantages of down-shifting which outweigh these drawbacks?

Parents

What will your parents say? They have seen you forge ahead in your career, and may well have seen your affluence as a source of security for you, your children and for them as they get older and face infirmity and expensive nursing bills.

They may well be unable to comprehend why you should wish to throw it all away – especially if you have never let them in on the miseries that your professional 'success' has brought you.

Peers

Your peers may be puzzled. They may try and portray you as someone who is burnt out – who is jumping before they are pushed. Can you handle that?

Think also about whether there are people you blame for your present predicament. Did you embark on the career you have come to hate to please your parents, or your partner? Do you resent your children for making it necessary for you to earn a large salary? If so, should you try to explain this to them, in order to try to diffuse any opposition they may express?

CHAPTER FOUR

Picking Your Portfolio
Establishing Your Goals

DOWNSHIFTERS believe that variety is not just the spice of life – it is the essential ingredient. The key problem among the overworked classes, from whose ranks downshifters are drawn, is that work is the cuckoo in the nest, pushing everything else out.

By now you will have come to firm conclusions about what is wrong with your job, about the reduced standard of living you are prepared to accept, and about the impact and benefits for personal relationships of the course of action you are considering.

The question now is, with what other things do you fill the rest of your life? How do you draw up your list of goals? How do you – to go back to a phrase used in Chapter 1 – establish your new 'portfolio career'?

The idea of establishing a portfolio career is that paid work becomes just one item within that portfolio, rather than the whole thing. Your life is a container and your job something held within it.

Now is the time to think about slotting into the portfolio the other things you wish to do with your time.

It might be helpful to think of your week in units. If you include commuting time and work done at home in the evenings or at weekends, your current working week probably takes up 50 or 60 hours (or units in this new way of reckoning) – perhaps more.

The portfolio approach to life means you can take these 60 units of available time and divide them up in a different way. Give, say, 25 units to work which would bring in the essential money, 10 to study, five for voluntary work, another 10 in improving the house – everything from painting and decorating to cleaning and gardening. That would leave five for you, to spend as you choose – reading, thinking, cycling in the country – anything you fancy. And you still have 10 units to devote completely to the children.

Of course, every downshifter will have their own very individual way of dividing their time, but what is striking is the way that, when you cut paid work down to size, so much time is left for other things.

Ian Callaghan left banking to buy a hotel on a remote Scottish island, a seasonal business which leaves seven months of the year free for his other interests.

Dennis Foster was working full-time running an old peoples' home with his wife Francesca. Now he works 25.5 hours a week as a community alarm service operator for Norwich City Council, and in his spare time has become a successful artist.

Peter Scott went part-time, job-sharing as a senior lecturer in computer programming at Sheffield Hallam University three days a week and devoting the rest of his time to local politics, renovating a house and gardening.

Essentially, by downshifting you are redesigning your whole life. You have given up the old framework of a 40-, 50- or 60-hour week in a job that lasted from the end of education until retirement at age 60 or 65.

If downshifting is to be a success for you personally, you must be sure you have a good idea of what you want to do and how to achieve it. You must have a realistic assessment of your skills, talents, interests and abilities. You must also have a good idea of what you want from life.

Those who downshift are usually looking for work that is useful and fulfilling in itself rather than in terms of what rewards it brings. Many people downshift in order to widen their range of activities, some of which will provide an income, some of which will not.

In subsequent chapters we will examine these options individually, and in greater detail, but first it is important for you to work out what the balance of activities should be for you. You may wish to work full-time but at a craft you have always enjoyed as a hobby – such as carpentry, pottery or gardening. You may already have discovered a local retailer who is keen to sell your work. But if there is one consideration that should be paramount for downshifters, it is to avoid the danger of exchanging one narrow, restricted lifestyle for another.

It would be worth the carpenter or potter considering if, perhaps, they would like to study part-time for that English degree they always wished they had taken, or devote one day a week to helping at – say – a local old peoples' day centre.

In building a portfolio that suits you personally, there are a number of areas you need to consider:

▼ What paid work do you want to do?
▼ Do you want to start a business?
▼ What voluntary work do you want to do?
▼ What new qualifications do you wish to acquire?
▼ Where do you want to live?

Let us look at these one by one.

Picking Your Portfolio, Establishing Your Goals

PAID WORK

There are many big questions here. For instance, can you stick with the same employer, or should you (or will you have to) switch employers? Should you switch careers? Many office workers are frustrated cooks, market gardeners, lumberjacks. Maybe there is even the odd lumberjack who would like to switch to corporate banking.

Whatever you want to do, the first criterion is finding work that will earn you the basic income to cover the standard of living that you have determined you need (Chapter 2 should have helped you to decide how much this is). Only you will know what the options are, given your personal skills and strengths. Careers guidance can be very useful because it gives an objective outsider's view of what your abilities are. But you also need something broader, a guide to your whole life, not just that slice in which you do paid work.

You are very likely to be switching from a staff position to a freelance one. You may be switching from working for a boss to being your own boss. You may be charging fees rather than drawing wages. Many downshifters who move from a staff job to what we can call a consultancy role find that they can earn, pro rata, far more than they did before. Because now, instead of selling their time at an hourly rate, or at a rate that is fixed through the imposition of a salary, they are selling their expertise. And expertise and time are more loosely related as a freelance than they are if you are on staff. In short, a consultant can charge a daily rate that is far higher than it would be if he or she were a permanent employee.

Many areas of work are being colonised by the self-employed as companies tend to concentrate on what they see as their core functions – the things that they are very good at – and leave other areas to those who specialise in them.

The ultimate handbook

If you charge by the hour you can only make more money by working longer hours. If you charge for the service that you provide, you can earn more while working fewer hours.

Many areas of work are now open to the freelance. From the professions to the craft skills, from accountancy to building, from public relations to the maintenance and repair of everything from kitchen appliances to cars. The farming out of subsidiary functions by companies has created a whole new area of freelance opportunities – from head-hunting to payroll to organising conferences. Then there are the support roles, such as gardeners, cooks and child-minders.

In all sorts of areas, the growth of freelance activities frees the individual to determine just how many hours he or she works a week, which makes downshifting a viable option for many, many people.

STARTING A BUSINESS

This is the dream of many downshifters, because it gives the greatest degree of freedom – although it also has the greatest element of risk attached to it. There is the possibility of total financial ruin. I know a former residential property owner who sold up and bought a café. He hates it and works 60 hours a week for no profit. But I also know a journalist who, feeling burnt out at 50, set up a small business creating in-house magazines, who has thrived.

VOLUNTARY WORK

To the downshifter, paid work's function is two-fold. First, of course, it brings in the money to keep you fed and the roof over your head. Secondly, it frees up some of your time, talent and expertise to offer free to those who need it.

Picking Your Portfolio, Establishing Your Goals

Voluntary work can be most valuable if you have a specific, and expensive, skill which an organisation or individual could not easily pay for but which they can greatly benefit from. Many downshifters have such skills.

A hard-pressed charity – for example – might find its income enormously boosted if it had created for it a professional – and free – advertising campaign. I know a market gardener who supplies her children's school so generously with plants that it won the local 'In Bloom' contest last year.

NEW QUALIFICATIONS

You might wish to turn a hobby into something which, eventually, could earn you money, or can help you save money by equipping you to, say, renovate the cheap, rundown but potentially splendid old house you have decided to move to when you downshift. You might wish to study for a qualification which will enhance your reputation within your profession, perhaps enabling you to work as a freelance, a consultant or simply for more money for fewer hours than you have to put in at the moment.

Studying, acquiring new knowledge or a new skill, is an excellent way to keep your spirits up if the rigours of downshifting begin to get you down. It is so clearly something positive, enriching and personally rewarding that it can help to make up for other hardships and setbacks.

CHOOSING WHERE TO LIVE

Can you do what you want to do where you live now, or must you move? Do you want to work at home or in an office? Maybe you can live in your dream location. I know downshifters who have first decided where they want to live, and only then thought about how they will make a living there. Often it is somewhere they grew up, or fell in love with in their youth – maybe it was the place they first gained independence, the town where they had their first job or went to university.

Many downshifters are determined to live in the country, or move abroad. Some see the remoter areas of Britain, say in Scotland, Cornwall or Wales, as the ideal place to downshift to.

The rise of computer communications has meant that for many people, location is now irrelevant to the job that they do. But that does not apply to everyone. And, in any case, locations that look wonderful on your summer holidays may be deathly in January.

One question may be nagging at you, as I know it has nagged at many of the downshifters I have interviewed: This portfolio business all sounds well and good, but how do I know what work is best for me – how can I be sure that my portfolio has the correct elements in it?

As I mentioned earlier, careers guidance may prove a good idea. But conventional careers guidance, which concentrates more or less solely on how you earn your living, is too narrow to be of full relevance to the downshifter.

Alexis Hallam, an occupational psychologist, specialises in helping clients to reach the correct conclusions about what work would suit them best. She is also a great proponent of the portfolio career:

A portfolio career is having a part-time employed job as one's main anchor and combining it with other working themes. You are designing in versatility.

Because the world is less certain, people are now having to manage change even more. There is often an opportunity for people to do things that they have always wanted to do. I advise people on how to make the transition.

I'm in the business of helping people to understand them-selves better in terms of their capability and natural aptitude, rather than what they are best at for one reason or another. Many people will become a lawyer or an executive because that is what they feel is best for them.

The tools of occupational psychologists are, in part, psy-chometric assessment. So we try to look at things objectively: measuring the person's aptitude, motivation, values, personal-ity – and that helps us a great deal with stereotypes about what people think they should be doing.

It helps me guide people in the right way, to help them manage appropriate changes.

Some people would go insane if they didn't modify their working life. I can see barristers who have a lot of qualifica-tions but are not earning a lot of money because they've never been fitted for the job aptitudinally.

One of our most famous examples was of a consultant surgeon who became a harp maker – very successfully.

Our case studies for this chapter created portfolios that really work for them.

Ian Callaghan and wife Jane lived in London. He had been a senior international banker with the Channel Tunnel project and then with the Storehouse group of high street shops which at the time included Habitat and BHS. Jane was working in antiques. They gave it all up to buy the Scarista House Hotel on the remote Hebridean isle of Harris.

The Channel Tunnel was a huge, complex job; a project which, if you are very lucky as a banker, you get once in a lifetime. After that I thought, 'I could do this for another 30 years and I'd never do anything as inter-esting again.'

In terms of banking there were no more challenges. Once you have done one major corporate financing you have done them all. They are not intellectually very interesting.

Jane had been working before our first baby, Charles, was born in 1988, but had not been at work for a couple of years by then. Alexander followed in 1995.

I suppose what made us want a new life was not so much the pressure of life in London, it was the thought of doing the same thing for 30 years. We felt there were other intellectual horizons, and from Jane's perspective there were many quality of life considerations.

The idea of having a small seasonal hotel arose because we wanted something that would give us a basic income for roughly half the year, so that we would have half the year free for other things. The main thing was to find a way of organising our lives with a great deal of variety built in. It was the life structure as much as the lifestyle that attracted us.

Other things have taken over more and more, so we are only open five months of the year now and occupy ourselves with a range of other activities the rest of the time.

We knew the hotel well and it had always been our ideal place. When we went on estate agents' lists we said ideally what we want is something like Scarista House in Harris – we didn't know it was for sale. Estate agents kept sending us roadhouses on the A74. We only by chance happened to see the last advert in the Financial Times *and offers closed about a week later, so we literally had a week to get an offer together. But we managed it. It all happened very quickly.*

Financially it was a risk. I'd just been head-hunted to join a major bank and that was a six-figure package,

Picking Your Portfolio, Establishing Your Goals

so it was a very big financial step to turn the offer down and come here instead. We didn't have to borrow heavily. We were selling a house in Islington, but we have a mortgage up here.

It was nerve-wracking. We arrived mid-March 1990 and opened for business in mid-April, never having done anything of the sort before. But we didn't particularly worry about it, we are both fairly friendly and hospitable types and we were pretty sure we could cook well enough to keep people happy.

Jane liked the idea of being involved in the business on the cooking side, so it was something we could be involved in together.

We are listed by Egon Ronay and Michelin. Guides just happen and are a complete lottery ... but it's nice to be in them.

We've done quite a lot of work – renovated right through inside. We started with eight bedrooms, now we are changing to a blend of hotel rooms and self-catering. We are small and basically fill up with a regular clientele.

We have never had any particular problems as outsiders on the island. I got very heavily involved quite early on in opposing plans to dig a superquarry which would have removed a huge chunk of a mountain, and I met and interacted with an awful lot of people, far more than I might have done otherwise.

That showed locals we had a deep concern for the place. I was always very open and straightforward about my reasons for opposing the scheme and a lot of people came round to my viewpoint. I started from a viewpoint of deeply distrusting multinational corporations, having worked for them myself, so I knew what the thinking was on the other side of the fence.

I have created an endurance race called the West-ern Isles Challenge. The race starts in Eriskay and works its way up the island chain to Butt of Lewis. Competi-tors travel by foot, mountain bike and canoe. We have attracted teams from the Metropolitan Police, the armed forces and City firms.

We hold it every year and it has established itself as the biggest event of its kind in the UK.

This year I am organising a very big programme marking the bicentenary of one of Britain's greatest natural historians – whom no one has ever heard of: a guy called William MacGillivray who was brought up on Harris. He went on to become professor of natural history at Aberdeen, he also wrote the first ever major history of British birds, he was a great animal painter, a mountaineer and just an extraordinary character. But one who has dropped out of sight completely. So we are putting together an exhibition which will tour the West-ern Isles, Aberdeen and the Highlands in the various venues he is associated with.

In terms of quality of life Harris certainly does meet all one's expectations. It is a very safe, clean place and from that point of view it is certainly something to thank your lucky stars for.

In terms of pressure I don't think it is all that dif-ferent. I've got the race and the MacGillivray both com-ing to a boil now so there is certainly lots going on all the time. It is not a quiet life and we weren't seeking one. We are both restless and energetic. One of the myths about small remote communities is that they are all inhab-ited by crofters who do nothing but smoke their pipes and reflect on this, that and the other all day. There are in fact plenty of young, energetic people who want these communities to thrive but retain the good things as well.

Picking Your Portfolio, Establishing Your Goals

It is certainly a struggle. The one big problem with the Western Isles is that it is entirely run by bureaucrats and quangos. Overcoming that is a bit of a nightmare.

Teleworking is a help for places like this, it's one of the most successful job sectors in the Western Isles. There are constantly being new jobs created. That's basically what I do; we put together the MacGillivray programme without me having really left the island thanks to computers.

Dennis Foster gave up full-time work running an old peoples' home with his wife Francesca, and now works for a local authority's alarm monitoring service for old people. The rest of the time he has devoted to becoming a successful artist.

I used to work 13 hours a day, six days a week for the princely sum of £7,000 a year. One day, stuck in a traffic jam, I thought 'Do I really want to do this for the next 20 years until I retire?'

I had always done art at evening classes and enjoyed it, but it became essential when I was made redundant. While my wife Francesca got a job as a warden in sheltered housing in Norwich I was unemployed, and art kept my head together.

One evening the teacher asked me where I had studied. I said I never had and she said 'Well, you ought to go.' I said it was impossible, that I had no money, but she told me I would get a grant. To humour her I applied to the school of art and design in Great Yarmouth and to my surprise I was accepted.

It was wonderful. My time there was like a gift I never thought I would have. It was like a holiday, being paid to do what I wanted to do. I learned more about myself than ever I did about art. But the grant

The ultimate handbook

only covered me for the two-year B-tech course, and I could not afford to go on to do a BA.

But, even so, after that, full-time work just did not appeal. And I looked around for work that would allow me to continue with my art.

The advertisement for an alarm operator sounded just right. We provide cover for 7,000 elderly or disabled people who live alone and may need support. They have alarm units they can press which act like a two-way radio. It is a 24-hour a day, 365-days a year service and we have a rolling shift system, with morning, afternoon and night shifts each week. This working arrangement suits me perfectly.

I started this job in 1990 and within six months I put on a one-man exhibition in Norwich with 54 paintings and about a dozen pieces of sculpture, all things I had done in my free time from the job. Previously I had worked for four and a half years and only done two paintings.

I took a cut in salary to start, but as the service got more successful and heavily used and the job got more demanding we got pay rises, so that now I am earning the most I have ever earned and working the fewest hours. I get around £12,000. You can live on that.

I couldn't have done it without my wife's support and willingness, or that of my daughter Emmalene who is 18 and studying theatrical stage management and lighting design.

Now, I cannot imagine any full-time job being good enough for me to consider changing my lifestyle. I love the way that work is not the be-all and end-all of my life. Fulfilment is more important. Unfortunately, in our society, work is the thing we are judged by. It's not who you are but what you do that counts with some people.

Picking Your Portfolio, Establishing Your Goals

Peter Scott is a senior lecturer in computer programming at the school of computing and management sciences, Sheffield Hallam University. He has been job-sharing for seven years, working three days a week in order to devote time to local politics, renovating a house and gardening.

I just decided that working full-time took up too much energy and creativity; there were other things I wanted to do. By Friday night I was tired and spent a lot of energy at the weekend getting ready for Monday again. Also I was trying to cram too much into the weekend because it would be over all too soon and you'd be back at work. It didn't seem balanced or sensible.

My wife Susan has a full-time job as a deputy head teacher and we have two teenage daughters; basically between us we were working too hard and didn't have enough time for other things.

One reason for going part-time was to leave time for my political activities. I am a member of the Green Party and I've campaigned for them and stood for them in the European elections. I don't believe in the conventional economics that the main political parties believe in. They all believe in economic growth and that it will bring more jobs. I look back to Harold Wilson's belief in technological revolution and the idea that technology is going to make life easy for us so that we will have more leisuretime. It didn't work then, in the sixties, and it is not going to work in the nineties.

Also, I'm doing up an old house and we have a large garden and I wanted to spend time on both. I enjoy physical work, it makes a change from writing and thinking and talking.

We had managed on one salary before when the girls were young and Susan gave up work, so we weren't worried about finances. What I initially tried to do wasn't very ambitious. All I asked was for my boss to let me go part-time, to give me a day a week to pursue my own interests. He wouldn't let me do that. He wanted everybody to be 100 per cent committed to work, as he saw it.

Eventually we managed to sort out the job-share with me and a colleague. I admit working part-time seemed odd to me when I first came across the idea. I was a very conventional person and when I first came across a man working part-time about six years ago I thought it was very strange, but when I came to know him it made sense. I realise now that his ideas were very green. He lived then the way I try to live now.

I don't know that attitudes have changed. I meet sympathetic people but I don't think it is a mainstream view.

My students assume that, because I am in computers, I spend the other two days a week out getting lucrative consultancy work. In fact I might spend the day cooking for the freezer or working in the garden.

Part of my reasoning was freeing work for somebody else. I think if we actually shared out the available work that wanted doing we could actually all get by on one or two days a week and have a much better life. Time to sing and dance and so on.

I certainly lead a greener lifestyle. For instance, around the house all the walls need replastering and rather than using a professional plasterer I am dry lining the walls so that they've got two and a half inches of fibre glass insulation in there. The rooms that have been dealt with are using a lot less heat. I'm doing labour-intensive work that would cost a fortune if I had to pay somebody to do it – not that I could afford to.

Picking Your Portfolio, Establishing Your Goals

You've got to be independent minded and not swallow all the consumerist propaganda that you get.

The difference it has made to us financially is not as great as we thought it would be. We have to think about things whereas before we didn't have to, but the only thing I can actually say we have definitely cut back on is we bought a used car instead of a new one. But we still go abroad for holidays and so on.

You can worry too much about financial things. If I got extra money I've no doubt I could spend it, but I wouldn't be any happier and I don't think the family would be any happier. I also realise that I'm in a lucky position. My wife has a well paid full-time job and doesn't want to work less because she enjoys it and doesn't feel that her employers would let her work part-time anyway.

Being a Green activist I know we can change the way we live our lives. When we talk about reducing energy and car usage people very often say it is impossible. The reason they say that is they assume society has to be organised and life lived as it is now. The Green Party says we must change the way we live. Consumerism isn't sensible, it's ludicrous. That everything we buy is made to fall to pieces and go out of fashion is crazy. If things were built to last and be repaired there would be a lot less work to do.

And then if the increased leisure were shared around instead of some people having more work than they want and no time for anything else while others have no work at all the world would be a better place.

The political parties talk about creating jobs. Well, in my department, we actually did it when I went part-time and somebody else got work. That is a job that would not have existed if I had not gone part-time. And *now I have time to do all sorts of other things that enrich my life – so two people gain greatly from one small decision.*

DECISIONS

Remember the categories we have run through in this chapter. As a reminder, here are each of the questions to consider again, and a pointer to the chapter that covers each one in more detail:

▼ What paid work do you want to do? *(see Chapter 5)*
▼ Do you want to start a business? *(see Chapter 6)*
▼ What voluntary work do you want to do? *(see Chapter 7)*
▼ What new qualifications do you wish to acquire? *(see Chapter 8)*
▼ Where do you want to live? *(see Chapter 9)*

Begin by writing down a statement on what you would like to do in each of these areas. At first, do not bother about being practical. Make a wish list.

Whatever the statements you make, they will begin to define the very important changes you have to make. They may be contradictory. You probably cannot, for instance, live in the Caribbean and start a company knitting traditional Shetland woolens. If you throw up contradictions you will need to reconcile them. You may have to go down your wish list and rate your desires with marks out of 10 to decide which are the most important to you and which can be discarded.

At the end of the exercise you should have a series of statements which will give you a template – a portfolio – which gives structure to your desire to downshift.

CHAPTER FIVE

Nice Work If You Can Get It

*And how an employer can help you
achieve your ambitions*

FINDING that essential core of money-earning work is, understandably, the hardest part of downshifting. With it, everything else slots into place. Without it, whatever you dreamed of cannot be financed.

Your existing employers could make things very easy for you – if they feel like it, or if you can convince them you are so valuable to the organisation that it is worth trying to accommodate your desire to reduce your workload.

If you are able to move seamlessly from full-time – or more than full-time – employment into some more flexible arrangement, then much of the fear and insecurity, much of the risk and uncertainty, is taken out of downshifting.

Pie in the sky? Certainly, there are many employers who do not have the flexibility, or the vision, to try to adapt their requirements so that they can be made to fit an employee's desire to downshift.

But, given the will, there are many ways that an employer can help, and avoid losing your valuable skills.

Some companies have an enviably good track record in this area. Lucas Industries, Boots the Chemist, National

Westminster Bank and the Inland Revenue are all recognised as being at the forefront in helping workers to adopt flexible working patterns.

There is also a charity called New Ways to Work whose *raison d'être* is to campaign for flexible work arrangements (*see* the Resources chapter). It receives 3,000 enquiries a year from individuals who wish to downshift and from companies who wish to respond to workers' desire for more free time without losing profits or competitiveness.

Among the different strategies New Ways to Work can advise upon are job-sharing, part-time working, term-time working, career breaks and working from home. jNew Ways to Work has been ground-breaking in that it has carried out extensive research into how these flexible working strategies can best be developed.

If your suspicion is that, in general, industry is opposed to downshifting, it is worth noting that New Ways to Work is supported by no less than the Director General of the Confederation of British Industry, Howard Davies. In the preface to *Balanced Lives*, an invaluable publication from the group, Davies says: 'The pressure of long hours on men is a serious problem, with insidious effects on family life. I have lived those problems myself. The answer is simple enough, you may think: just go home. But to men under pressure at work that is not useful advice. More sophisticated strategies are needed to reconcile the often conflicting demands of work and family life.'

By all means assume the worst when you approach your employer to ask for new working arrangements, but be prepared also to be pleasantly surprised. One thing that has struck me as I have interviewed a wide range of downshifters is that many of them found that, once their employer was convinced that they really would quit if their working hours and arrangements could not be adapted in some significant way, many bent over backwards to keep them.

Throughout this book there are dozens of case studies on people who have radically altered the way in which they earn their money, who have gone from accountancy to viniculture or from banking to the church. But here, just for a change, I will concentrate on three people who have downshifted within their existing careers – and with great success.

Simon and Brigit Wilkinson job-share as general practitioners in rural Yorkshire.

Julian Duxfield is employee development manager for the Unilever-owned company Lever Industrial. He took a two-year career break at the age of 30 to travel extensively and study for an MSc in industrial relations and personnel management.

Martin Rathfelder is a welfare rights officer for Manchester City Council. When he was widowed his employer responded to his desire to bring up his two children by himself and to continue in his job by allowing him to work at home for part of the week.

Of course, it is not possible in three short personal accounts to describe the many and varied ways in which employees have managed either to reduce their hours or take a break from their careers temporarily. One person who has close personal experience of the full range of flexible working arrangements is Charlie Monkcom, who works three days a week for New Ways to Work. He says:

New Ways to Work was set up to challenge the 40-hour monolith in a hundred different ways. We produce examples to show it can work in other ways. We are a campaigning organisation, trying to change the way the world works.

One way we tend to do that is by providing very specific, real examples of good practice, of different ways of working that are actually functioning satisfactorily.

Charlie says attitudes to flexible working have changed radically in the 20 years that New Ways to Work has been in existence.

We were set up in 1977, and in the early days there was a lot of resistance to what we were advocating. Some of it came from employers who could see nothing in it for them, some from trade unions which did not like what they saw as an attack on the principle of full-time working.

In the first half of the eighties, long before the concept of downshifting had gained popular acceptance, we were working with individuals to help them persuade employers that flexible working was a viable option.

Things really began to change in the late eighties, when you had more and more people, mainly women, saying they wanted to get the work and family thing into some kind of balance. You had interest from employers because of a Government report on the declining number of school leavers. This trend meant that employers realised they were faced with going out and finding new sources of workers. They looked particularly for women to take the place of school leavers – women returners who had given up work some time earlier for family or other reasons.

What had also happened was that some people who shared our views had moved into positions of influence within companies – in personnel departments in particular – and were beginning to be listened to.

Also, employers started to come to us for advice on setting up flexible working schemes. There was the Midland

Bank with its child-care scheme, which enabled women to tailor their working hours to their family commitments. Boots introduced a job-share policy. It was all focused around women, and keeping them in employment. The banks introduced all sorts of career break schemes.

So there was a certain amount of public acceptance of the idea that work didn't need to be done in 40-hour chunks.

In the nineties we have been getting a lot more enquiries from men. For years it was 9 to 1 women to men, now it is far more equal. Men may still find it harder to change to a flexible way of working than women do. Nevertheless, I think the trend is pretty much unstoppable. Certainly many more men are now choosing to change something in their working lives, deciding it is not worth working 60 hours a week. Some say bugger this I want to do something else – climb mountains or something, work with Oxfam in Africa for a year. Not everybody wants a linear career.

But although attitudes are now less strongly against flexible working, we still get a lot of enquiries from people who want to work part-time but are not being allowed to by their employers for one reason or another.

We advise them on which arguments to use, and give them specific examples of other people in a similar work situation to them where flexibility has worked perfectly well, to the benefit of the employer as well as to the employee.

I think the argument is beginning to be won with employers. An increasing number of employers have learnt they can offer a 30-hour week and the organisation won't seize up, and that people will work perhaps harder and more efficiently if you cut their working hours.

So, New Ways to Work are of great help if you believe you can downshift with your existing employer. But what if that is not possible? What if you want to continue in your current line of work, but will have to do so either by switching companies, or by going freelance?

Organisations are coming into existence which have been set up to help professionals in specific disciplines to work flexibly, to crack the code and find work that is of the kind they want, and of which there is neither too much nor too little.

For example, Gay Haines, chief executive of the advertising head-hunters Kendall Tarrant, was so convinced of the growth of downshifting that she helped establish a new sister company called Scala, which caters to the needs of people who want to move away from conventional, full-time employment.

We were finding that more and more of the top creative people were choosing to split their lives ... to spend part of their life writing a book or a script or directing a film, and the other part of their life financing those projects by working in advertising or marketing or whatever.

It is a more intelligent route because those people with a specific talent can sell their services for individual projects to agencies or organisations that might not be able to afford them on a full-time basis. For employers, it is simply the most effective use of human resources; why should a company bear the burden of the full-time salary of specialists they can employ as and when they need them?

We set out to support creative and media downshifters in rather the way that a barrister's chambers does – where you have 40 people working independently but being managed by a clerk.

Downshifting is a positive trend for everybody. We hope to expand to take on other professions. This is not a temporary fashion; to my mind there is no doubt that by the end of the century, half of all working people will be leading their lives in this way.

Scala's managing partner, John Stuart, explains exactly how the organisation can help downshifters:

Advertising suffered terribly in the recession, with the consequence that the most experienced people – who are inevitably the most expensive – were sacked. I estimate around 20 per cent of creatives were forced out.

We act as strategic planners who analyse markets on behalf of advertising companies. They phone us with a brief for a particular project, and we find the most suitable person on our books who fits the bill.

Some of these people are financially driven, in that they need to keep working to fund the lifestyle they enjoyed in the boom years of the eighties. However, increasingly, many people have simply been driven out by the politics of the industry.

Previously, clients made a commitment to a particular agency and spent huge sums of money on projects. But now, companies are prepared to spend less money and commission smaller ads.

Many women in the industry have chosen to go freelance because they want to have families and prefer the flexibility of working at home. Agencies have become increasingly aware of costs and are contracting out work to freelances. There is a large pool of extremely talented people who are available for work. Scala effectively manages the careers of freelances and is able to tailor the requests of agencies by analysing their brief and selecting the best candidate. Freelances are able to work effectively from all over the country with the new technology on offer. Most of them have Apple Macs and dedicated phone lines which enable

Nice Work If You Can Get It

them to deliver strategic work direct to the commissioning agencies.

We now have people on our books from as far away as Cornwall and Somerset. In all we have about 175 creative people serving about 30 to 40 agencies. And the numbers are growing.

We also have a number of international agencies, especially in Switzerland, who acknowledge that British is Best and come to us with work.

Also, we are finding that more people are downshifting into different [albeit] related areas. With the increasing amount of contracted-out programmes on television, we are finding creative people are moving into scriptwriting, book writing and radio work. These are the sorts of people who were never really satisfied with office-based work, and they are happier to move from job to job.

Let's look at our case studies in detail.

Husband and wife Simon and Brigit Wilkinson are GPs sharing a rural practice in Yorkshire.

Only in 1990 did the GP contract change and it became possible for doctors to job-share. Brigit and I come as an entity, we applied as an entity. When we were applying, two and a half years ago, it was uncommon to see jobs saying 'job-share considered'. Everyone was advertising for a full-time GP to replace an outgoing partner or as an extra partner. We applied saying we are two people to fill one slot. This is our first permanent position in general practice, but we had locumed before.

Job-sharing is very noticeably less novel now. Now you see a tremendous number of ads saying 'job-share considered' in the British Medical Journal.

The pressure for job-share has come from doctors themselves. People are fed up of doing 80-hour weeks. And some of the pressure is from the top end, say GPs in their mid-fifties who don't want to retire but don't want to do the 80 hours and all the on-call work. Quite a number of older GPs want to work half-time, and that leaves vacancies for other half-timers to come in. And it makes people realise working part-time is not too bad at all. It is not too complicated, it doesn't mean they are slack or don't consider their work important.

Some of the pressure is to get women into general practice because there is a very big shortage of female GPs and people have realised that a lot of women don't want to work full-time so, to some extent, they have had to accept the only way they are going to get a woman is to get somebody job-sharing like us, which is still very rare, or to get two half-time women job-sharing.

It is much easier to be a good doctor when you are working half the hours. I work Mondays, Fridays and every other Wednesday, so on my weeks when I'm off Tuesday, Wednesday and Thursday by the time I get back to work on a Friday morning after spending three days at home with two kids I am actually quite keen to get back to work – whereas everybody else is knackered and looking forward to the end of the week.

I think it makes me a much better doctor, and a much better father as well because I would frankly go mad if I had to stay at home five days a week looking after the children all the time. We have two pre-school age daughters, Anna and Eleanor. I need to get out and stimulate my brain a bit. But I would get bored with general practice, doing it all day every day.

It's a nice quiet little backwater where we live. Market Wheton itself is a small town of 4,500 people

Nice Work If You Can Get It

and we are 20 miles from a town of any size. It's not classically beautiful so we don't get hordes of tourists, and a traffic jam is getting stuck behind a tractor on the way to work. It's a very nice place to bring up children.

There are three full-time doctors in the practice, all male, and us two. It is largely up to us how we split our duties. We don't have any appointments in the practice so people are used to turning up, finding out who is on duty and seeing whom they want to see that day.

We share a number of patients, but not all of them. If they want to see one of us rather than the other they know exactly when each of us is around. Communication between Brigit and I is important. I might come home on a Monday and say I saw Mrs So and So today and I think it might be this, so I've asked her to come in tomorrow. Brigit is then fully briefed and can take up with the patient where I left off.

It is very easy, there have been no problems. Patients accept it like ducks to water. I thought, particularly in a remote rural area, they might be a bit phased by the idea of a husband and wife job-sharing, but it hasn't been a problem for them at all.

There seems no point in having children if you never see them. I know a lot of our contemporaries who are GPs who go out at 7, back at 7 and if they have young children they are in bed, so they don't see them from one week's end to the next. It seems pointless.

Also, when the children are older there are plenty of things outside medicine that I want to do. At the moment I go to a gardening course on the days when the older one is at nursery because that interests me. I would like to do a part-time degree course when they are older and off my hands during the day. I was thinking only the other week – what if I took a garden design *course and then if I got bored with general practice I would have an alternative career lined up.*

Thanks to the job-share I am able to have a much more varied life. We could both work full-time, farm the kids out to child-care and have no time to spend the money. You only get one go at life and there seems no point in working like a dog until you are 65 to die at 67 in a really big, empty house.

There are no drawbacks really. Financially it is just something you get used to. GPs earn a good salary and we can survive off one income. It is a question of cutting your cloth. We know what we earn and live within it.

But people do treat you differently in a job-share. They are used to women working half-time, but not men. They look at you as if wondering 'What's wrong with him if he only wants to work half-time?' They question your masculinity for a start. This doesn't give me big psychological problems, though.

People sometimes treat you as though you are not 100 per cent committed to your job – and frankly I'm not. I'm 100 per cent committed to my family and my job is a way of supporting my family. I enjoy my job but if something has to give it is going to be the job rather than the family.

I think there should be a lot more people who are not so committed to their jobs that the rest of their life goes out the window.

I think job-sharing is the way forward for work, partly because ultimately it is a more equitable way of distributing work. I can't foresee a time when there will ever be full-time employment again and this is a way of distributing the work that is there to be done among the people who are there to do it. It does mean people are going to have to accept that there will be a lower standard

Nice Work If You Can Get It

of living financially, but a much higher quality of life.

I can't imagine going back to full-time work. The idea appals me.

A lot of people say to me, 'Well, I can see how it would work in your job but it wouldn't work in mine – I have got too much to do.' But they don't realise you are not doing a full job in half the time, you are doing half a job.

It also means you suddenly realise that the world goes on without you at work. Nobody likes to realise they are dispensable, but they all are, none of us works 24 hours a day every day. We are all part-time anyway.

Julian Duxfield is employee development manager for the Unilever company Lever Industrial, which employs 800 staff. He was a personnel manager when, at the age of 30, he decided to take a two-year career break in order to travel extensively and study for an MSc in industrial relations and personnel management at the London School of Economics. He has a partner, Lucy, and a daughter, Isobel.

In the whole history of the career break scheme we have only had two men on it. Women use it for maternity reasons, even though it is open for men or women to take for family or further education reasons.

You step out of a job for a couple of years, so you are not getting the same work experience. It may be providing you with valuable personal experience but you are not actually getting experience that people who remain in the job are gaining. So undoubtedly you are going to put your career back.

That said, the Masters degree was a clear personal benefit to me and my ability to do jobs in the future, my marketability as a personnel manager.

The less tangible part was the travelling. I felt if I was ever going to do it that was the right stage to do it. My partner, Lucy, who is a journalist, took a career break at the same time. We started on the first of January and travelled for the first six months around southeast Asia, China, Pakistan. Then I did some mountaineering in Europe over the summer.

I started my Masters course at the London School of Economics in September and that carried on through to the following September. Then I went out to Nepal mountaineering for two months. I was back at work on the first of December.

The break was fantastic – we undertook the trips of a lifetime. We saved for a year to be able to take the break, and I know that such trips will be impossible in the future. Four months ago we had our first child. We knew we wanted children and hoped it would be possible, and you can't travel in the way we did when you have kids.

I haven't seen any evidence of other men in the company thinking of following my example. The reactions have been interesting. Some people said you are totally bonkers – this was more before I left – and said 'What are you doing that for? You are chucking your career in, it is a huge risk, you are not going to find work when you get back,' all these apocalyptic predictions.

And the other reaction was 'That's great, I wish I had done it when I was your age.' So there were two extremes, two very polarised views.

There was no guarantee that a job would be waiting at the end of the break, but I didn't have a problem as it turned out. In the summer of my degree I was looking around to see what was available. I was quite keen to get back into Unilever if there was the right opportunity for me, and this job looked like the right opportunity.

Quite a lot of blue-chip companies do have career break schemes now. It is a very low-risk thing for a company to have, especially if there is no guaranteed return ticket at the end. The company is keeping in touch with the employee, who leaves to do whatever, and if they want to attract that employee back they can stand a good chance of doing so, and for very little commitment on their behalf. Realistically, though, very few companies can absolutely guarantee you a job back at the end of it.

If companies haven't got a scheme they should think very seriously about putting one in operation. And that they are used by people who really want to use them, not because they've been pushed into using them.

Career breaks here [at Unilever] are for a maximum of five years, a minimum of one year; we try to keep in touch my getting people to do work on a consultancy basis for four weeks of each year they are away. The key thing is that you keep in touch with what is happening in the company. I didn't do any work but I kept in touch with my ex-boss. I didn't want my old job back but he was able to keep me informed of other vacancies around the company. The job I now have is at the head office. My responsibility is to work with the personnel managers and directors in the various Unilever companies, helping them to deliver equal opportunities policies.

Taking a break really does rejuvenate you and help you think through your priorities.

If I had said I wanted to take two years off to go travelling I think it would have been harder to gain *acceptance within the company. But the fact I was doing the MSc in one of the years off made it acceptable.*

Martin Rathfelder is a welfare rights officer for Manchester City Council. He is widowed with two children: Katy (11) and Emily (8). He works from home part of the time.

I used to have two jobs, both of which I shared with a friend called Clive. One was as a welfare rights officer, advising patients at Manchester Royal Infirmary about what benefits they were entitled to claim, the other was for a small computer software firm called Ferret.

For Ferret we were developing software with which welfare entitlements could be worked out. There was a lot of travelling involved. I might have to get up at 5 a.m. to go to Cardiff.

Then my wife became very ill with cancer. At the same time Ferret offered me a full-time job, but I thought 'I can't spend all week shooting round the country when I could be needed at home at any time.' So I got Clive's full-time job as a welfare rights officer and he went to Ferret.

When my wife died in 1993 I obviously had to have work which would fit in with my commitments to the girls.

In the process of going full-time for the council I escaped from ordinary restrictions on the hours I work in the office at the Infirmary. There is no clocking on or off at the hospital, there is just me there. My boss is very tolerant, he doesn't mind much what hours I do so long as I am doing a reasonable amount of work. If the children are ill or something has to be seen to, like the gas man coming, then I stay at home and work.

In fact I probably do more than the 35 hours I am supposed to.

I effectively do two jobs. I give advice to individuals who have problems with their social security, I write letters for them, represent them at tribunals and put pressure on various officials. My other job is in computer development for the advice service, which I largely do at home. It is the problem-solving side of computers. I run a large data base collecting the results of all case work the advisers do in the city. In order to do that I require a bit of peace and quiet, which is more easily come by at home than in the office.

I tell people to ring me at home and even if I am doing something else I will talk to them because computer problems need to be sorted out while they are happening.

The work is very important to me, and never more so than when my wife was dying. Not just because I needed the money but in keeping my head together. It was completely stress free. I didn't want to stop working, but I had to do work which allowed me to look after the kids as well.

If my boss had not been so flexible I would have had to leave the job. I discovered after some time that he had got no official permission for the working arrangement I had agreed with him. There were some worries expressed. Some people said what if all single parents who work for the council found out what you are doing...?

The beauty of it is the work divides itself, I have to see the public, which must be done at the office, then there is the computer work which is behind the scenes, self-directed. I couldn't do that side of the work in the Infirmary where I deal with patients all the time.

The problem with working from home occurs not for the individual, but for that person's manager. Your boss has to trust you. I could be going fishing. If you are there sitting in front of them in an office they have the security of seeing you actually at work – but you could be present yet not working. What does an employer want – time or results? That is easy in a job where you can measure results, but often you can't. I get results – does it matter if I'm in the office for only 30 hours and others are there longer, as long as the job gets done?

It is not just the individual who benefits from flexible working. One of the strongest arguments in favour of downshifting is that, properly managed, it can have advantages for employers. New Ways to Work also believe that there are benefits for Government and society in general. Such an argument may not cut much ice with the hatchet-faced company man who holds your future in his hands, but it should help reassure downshifters that they are not being purely selfish.

Here are New Ways to Work's general guidelines on flexible working patterns as they apply to individuals, organisations, Government and society:

▼Individuals should think laterally and flexibly; they may be surprised to find that their proposal to work reduced or more flexible hours is easier to negotiate than they thought. On an employee's side is the fact that flexible employment is needed to meet the changing demands of customers, and an individual's ability to balance the customers' needs with their own requirements will strengthen a downshifter's case.

▼Organisations need to recognise that long hours and stressed employees do not result in high-quality, effective outputs. They should create a healthier working environment which provides opportunities for flexibility and for employees to lead more balanced lives.

▼ Government should provide a legal framework which acknowledges that both men and women have an equally important role to play in caring responsibilities.

▼ Society should ask what happened to the leisure society so talked about 20 years ago. What happened to quality of life? Why is the reality that so many people in employment are working longer hours than they were while so many others are unemployed? It is healthier for society, for business and for individuals to change things.

The fact that there are benefits from downshifting that are felt by people other than the downshifter is surely one of the strongest arguments in its favour.

If downshifters make better – not worse – employees, then surely downshifting is something an employer should encourage?

In their book *Balanced Lives*, New Ways to Work say that men who work flexibly have increased motivation and energy. This is positive for both them and their employers. They argue that we now need a different measure of commitment at work which considers an individual's output rather than just the visible time they spend in the workplace.

Professor Cary Cooper, pro-Vice Chancellor at the University of Manchester Institute of Technology and a distinguished organisational psychologist, has coined the term 'presenteeism', the opposite of absenteeism, to characterise the myth that hours served equal work done.

He argues that, for too long, the assumption has been that long hours equate with productivity. If you are working on a production line, where a machine dictates your speed of

The ultimate handbook

work, that might be the case. But the argument does not hold with more flexible types of work. He argues that long hours spent in the office might be seen as a sign of inefficiency, rather than of dedication.

He also argues that long hours cause stress, and stressed employees are not the best workers to have.

According to the International Labour Office, the effects of stress at work are thought to cost up to 10 per cent of Gross National Product in Britain. The Health and Safety Executive estimate that a total of 40 million working days per year are lost in the UK due to stress-related illness.

Prof Cooper is an expert on stress. At business conferences he tells bosses how much the stress caused by long working hours is costing them in commercial terms. Britons, he points out, work the most hours in Europe, while the Germans work the fewest. So how can it be, he asks, that long hours are good for British companies but short hours are good for German ones?

He argues in favour of several kinds of flexibility. On working hours, for example, he points out that commuting, especially when the time is spent fuming in a traffic jam, is a very unproductive way of spending time. So why not let workers stagger their hours? Do a couple of hours at home first thing, then travel to the office at 11?

And to counter presenteeism, he suggests employers set a target for how much work is to be done, and leave it up to the employee where it is done and how long it takes.

While the chance to look out on your garden while you work, and to spend your lunch hour relaxing in it, has obvious attractions for the downshifter, it is important to recognise the wider benefits of home working.

The reality that so many workers can now work from home – and that the home can be anywhere – has enormously beneficial social implications. It can mean the end to the dominance of Southeast England over the rest of the country. It can mean that talented people do not have to leave their remote communities in order to find fulfilling work. Instead, fulfilling work can be brought to them.

For example, Donnie Morrison is from the Western Isles but had to leave to find work. Recently he returned as an expert in information technology for the local council and enterprise board, and has brought a wide range of highly skilled work to the islands, thanks to computer technology.

Fifteen people on the islands of North and South Uist and Benbecula can work from their homes, pouring information down the electronic superhighway. The initiative is bringing work and prosperity to one of Britain's more depressed regions.

The 15 workers cull articles from business journals, reducing and indexing them to a common format for a company that sells a reference service to subscribers.

Mr Morrison says: 'This type of work means we can at last make proper use of the islanders' skills. We have more graduates per head of population than any other part of the UK but it is difficult for them to find work here. I have people with fantastic qualifications that they cannot use working on fish farms. They want to live here but have had to leave in the past because there is no suitable work.'

Other projects are on the go. Mr Morrison has compiled a register of over 200 people able to provide a range of office skills, computer programming, specialist research and translation services in Russian, Norwegian, French, German, Spanish and Gaelic. He also competes with the temporary secretary market in London. There, temps cost £16 a day and take up office space. He can offer a temp whenever he or she is wanted by an employer, via computer, at a fraction of the cost.

Sharing available work among more people by reducing the hours each works is another policy that can help society. As a consequence, fewer people need claim state benefits and fewer become depressed and alienated and lose their sense of self-worth.

Here, mainland Europe is way ahead of Britain.

At Volkswagen in Germany nearly 100,000 workers agreed to reduce their weekly hours from 36 to 28.8. For this 20 per cent cut in hours they took a 15 per cent cut in pay. The company say it saved 20,000 jobs. And those doing the jobs had more free time to themselves and to devote to their families.

In France there are a growing number of examples showing that reducing and rearranging work hours can lead to more jobs being created.

At Hewlett Packard's computer plant near Grenoble the working week was cut from 39 to 33 hours with no pay cut, but in return the staff had to be very flexible about what hours they worked and when. The week could be between 25 and 46 hours as required. The deal meant 100 jobs were created.

Brioche Pasquier, a baker based near Nante, hired 220 new workers at its nine plants, bringing its total workforce up to 1,250, following an agreement with workers that they would reduce the working week from 39 hours to 33.25, but annualised, so that workers put in more hours when demand is high and take more time off when it flattens.

The argument in favour of flexible working was perhaps best summed up by French economist Alain Grielen in his book *Today's Unemployment: Sign of a New Era?* He believes that if European jobs kept disappearing because of increased productivity and competition from low-wage countries, purchasing power could only be maintained by increasing handouts to the jobless. It would mean maintaining full-time jobs for a diminishing part of the population while paying more and more to the rest in unemployment benefits. No, he said, the better alternative is job-sharing.

While those who downshift are undoubtedly thinking of themselves and their own welfare to a large degree, many downshifters also have an unselfish motive. Many of those I spoke to in the course of researching this book said that one of the things that motivated them to reduce their working hours was the feeling that work is inequitably shared and that if you are working all the hours God sends you are depriving others of work that could be theirs.

The experts agree. Pamela Meadows, director of the Policy Studies Institute, says the most important problem facing society today is how to find work for those who want it, how to reduce the hours of those who have too much, and how to make us believe our jobs have a future.

In many cases, downshifting can provide the solution.

DECISIONS

▼ Can you persuade your existing employer to allow you to work flexibly?

▼ Can you find more suitable work with another employer?

▼ Should you go freelance, selling your services to a range of employers?

▼ Can you do your job from home? Would you like to?

The ultimate handbook

CHAPTER SIX

Taking Care of Business

IF YOU plan to start a business, the style of downshifting you are contemplating is distinctly different to that of the portfolio-builder who wants to ensure that paid work does not take up the majority of his or her time.

As Fiona Aitken, whose story is featured in Chapter 1, described to me so vividly, starting a business is not opting out, it is very much opting *in* to the mainstream.

Having your own business can easily mean that you have as much responsibility on your shoulders as before – probably a great deal more. The difference will be that you are your own boss: you decide what you do and when, you call the shots. Like any other downshifter, you are going after fulfilment.

For many people contemplating going into business for themselves, as David Lavarack, Small Business Services Director for Barclays Bank says, 'the desire to be their own boss and start up in business stems from a strong sense of independence and self-reliance.' Qualities the downshifter has in abundance.

Almost one in six Britons in employment – 16 per cent – have seriously considered starting a business. The majority –

75 per cent – put their thoughts into action. One in eight workers are now out on their own.

Nevertheless, it could be argued that the best advice if you want to start a business is: Don't. Because, while business start-ups are at record levels, business failures remain very high too. While nearly half a million new businesses are started each year in the UK, the number of business failures annually is within a few tens of thousands of that figure. And, for every 10 new businesses that are started today, four will have failed within three years.

Nevertheless, there are still about 2.7 million businesses in this country, and two-thirds of them employ only one or two people. Which means that it is perfectly possible to start and run a successful small business. The trend is very much towards fewer large corporations and more small businesses, for all the reasons that we have explored in this book so far. As large firms downsize – sack people, in plain language – as they contract out activities which are peripheral to their main sphere of business, and as telecommunications make it possible for more and more people to work anywhere they fancy, the number of small, one- or two-person businesses will continue to grow.

Surveys also show that, these days, many people start their business while still employed full-time by a company. This is a classic downshifter's strategy. It gives you time to ensure that your business idea is a viable one, and that you like working at it, before you burn your bridges.

The range of businesses which downshifters start is an incredibly wide one – as diverse, indeed, as are the people who downshift.

David Jenkins gave up his job as an accountant working abroad in Italy to buy and run an English vineyard.

Emma-Louise Salter gave up her career as a chef to train as a practitioner in vacuflexology – a branch of alternative medicine. She now has her own one-woman business.

Pat and Tony Brown gave up their jobs as – respectively – manager of a plant-hire firm and teacher to run a bed-and-breakfast in rural mid-Wales.

The most common age at which people start new businesses also happens to coincide with the key years for downshifting. Thirty-nine per cent of all new businesses are started by people between the ages of 25 and 34. This, say Barclays, who commissioned the survey, reflects a more measured and cautious approach adopted by those seeking to start up in business, with people waiting to gain employment experience before going it alone.

There are more women starting businesses, too. The figure is up from 25 to 27 per cent, which is said to reflect the healthier financial climate in which the sort of businesses women tend to start – retailing, catering and leisure – are aided by the rise in consumer spending.

More people are starting their new businesses from home, in classic downshifting style. From March 1994 to December 1995 the percentage doing so rose from 33 to 41 per cent.

There is also research which shows that older people who start businesses have a better chance of making them succeed than younger people. In the study 'New Firms and their Bank', conducted by Robert Cressey and Professor David Storey at Warwick University Business School's Centre for Small- and Medium-Sized Enterprises, it was concluded that by far the most important factor in determining survival is the age of the founder of a business. The study found that businesses started by people aged between 50 and

55 were more than twice as likely to survive than those begun by those aged between 20 and 25.

There are two reasons for this, according to Storey. The first is that young people do not have the experience and business knowledge needed to survive in a competitive environment. The second reason is – significantly for the downshifter – job prospects.

'If you are between 50 and 55, you have to stick with it because your chances of getting a job are much lower. If you are 20 to 25, you have less stickability because there is a better chance of returning to employment.'

There are two ways of looking at the above comment. You can either find it depressing – that older people are forced to grind away at a failing business until the bitter end – or encouraging, as the better figures for business survival for the older entrepreneur mean that while, in general, age is a disadvantage in the employment market, when starting your own business it is a positive asset.

As so many who downshift are doing so partly because they see diminishing employment prospects as they get older, it is encouraging to realise that your age actually equips you to start your own business. At last! A reason to look forward to getting old – for the downshifter at least.

Small businesses are the backbone of the British economy, generating ideas, innovation and jobs. The owners of small businesses are highly individual, and the key to their success is commitment and creativity. They stake everything on their businesses and naturally take tremendous pride in their achievements.

But ...

There is a downside to working for yourself. You have to face the fact that your dream could become a nightmare. It will help if you do not expect to become rich and, indeed, if making money ranks lower than satisfaction and fulfilment on your list of priorities. As a downshifter, you should be better equipped in this than, perhaps, the average company-founder might be. Nevertheless, you should bear in mind that there is growing evidence that working for yourself is not a route to riches.

Anne Corden of the University of York has studied the question of pay and self-employment and says: 'The huge growth in self-employment, including home working, has generated low incomes and an increasing need to claim means-tested benefits such as Family Credit.' She adds 'Combining work with family responsibilities can be very difficult.'

Ms Corden says that the self-employed are treated as second-class citizens by home loan companies, insurers, Government departments and by some of the firms who use their labour. For example, if you want a mortgage as an employed person you are eligible once you can prove your income. As a self-employed person you will normally need to provide a three-year accounting record to prove what you are worth.

As another example, being self-employed reduces the range of pension arrangements open to you. You do not have the option of joining a company scheme, nor are you eligible for the State Earnings Related Pension Scheme (SERPS). And even personal pensions, which often require a degree of earnings predictability that you may not be able to guarantee, can prove to be a headache.

While the risks of business failure remain high, there is much that you can do to cut the chances of failure. There are several sources of sound business advice, ranging from banks, accountants and solicitors to the DTI-sponsored chain of local advice centres called Business Links. In partnership with chambers of commerce, training and enterprise councils, local authorities, enterprise agencies and the private sector, the Business Link chain is a high-tech source of advice,

Taking Care of Business

consultancy and inter-business networking. Business Links are 'one-stop shops' offering a single source of advice for the nation's small businesspeople.

There are many other sources of information, and their use to you will depend on exactly what business you are starting. A full list of contacts and addresses is included in the Resources chapter at the end of this book.

Many people go to their local bank. If you want to raise money to finance your venture, you may have no choice. But if you don't have to borrow, you are in a far stronger position.

Whenever I have spoken to downshifters who have started their own businesses, the question of how well or badly their local bank has treated them always comes up. Many found themselves unhappy with the way they were dealt with.

The Federation of Small Businesses was so concerned at the power the banks have over their members' enterprises that it commissioned a report on the subject, and came to the conclusion that the banks have a stranglehold on the small businesses which borrow from them.

The report warns that, in general, small businesses are not generating the profits needed to become self-sufficient, and that more than half rely on overdrafts and other non-fixed forms of financing.

Tony Miller, chairman of the Federation's financial affairs division, says: 'Only as alternative methods of self-financing and profit retention are developed will small business move from this vulnerable position.'

This means that the 50 per cent of small businesses which are not beholden to the banks are in a far stronger position than those which are. So, if you can avoid borrowing to achieve your downshifting dream, do, even if you have to delay making your break – a subject which we will look at fully in Chapter 11.

The ultimate handbook

Even if you are not borrowing, I still think it is worth popping into your high street bank. All the banks boast of how friendly they are to small businesses, and the literature they publish to guide you towards coming up with a business that will succeed can be very useful.

NatWest, for example, prefaces its 'Business Start Up Guide' with a handy questionnaire to help you decide if you are cut out to start a business. You are asked to tick a series of 16 characteristics. If you can honestly tick all 16, say NatWest, you have got what it takes:

1 I am realistic about my capabilities.
2 I am self-disciplined and I do not let things drift.
3 I have the full support of my family.
4 I am ready to put in seven days a week, if necessary.
5 I can get on well with people.
6 I can make careful decisions.
7 I can cope under stress.
8 I do not give up when the going gets tough.
9 I can learn from my mistakes.
10 I can take advice.
11 I am patient, and I expect a long haul.
12 I can motivate people.
13 I am in good health.
14 I am enthusiastic.
15 I know about the risks.
16 I have specific aims.

Even if you are unsure whether to start a business or not, getting this material, and the forms on which they invite you to present your business plan, can be enormously helpful. Filling in a business plan will help you to see just how sound (or half-baked!) your business idea is.

Whichever business plan guide you use, from whatever bank or other financial organisation, all will ask you to plan ahead, stating your ultimate goal for your company and what you expect to achieve in your first, second, third year and so on.

It will ask you for evidence that you know your market, and that you describe your potential customers. It will ask you to describe the product or service you intend to offer, to determine the price you intend to sell it at, its quality and how you intend to establish your reputation as a trader. You will be asked, among other things, to state what advertising you will undertake, how you will deliver your goods, where your business will be located and what after-sales service you will provide.

You will be asked to compare your product or service with that offered by one, two or more local competitors. How will you be better than them? Will you be cheaper? Will you offer a better product or quality of service?

You will be asked to price your product, assessing all your overheads and then establishing your break-even point – the point at which you move into profit.

You will be asked to justify your sales projections and to detail what firm orders you already have, to define how your books will be kept and to say how you intend to raise the finance that you need.

Being forced to do all this is a real eye-opener.

The logic in preparing a business plan is clear. In doing so you are setting out your objectives and outlining what you hope to achieve. You therefore have something to measure up to.

If you have a plan in existence you can refer to it regularly, measuring your progress against it and acknowledging when you need to revise your ambitions. Having a plan laid out will also help you to persuade a bank manager, accountant

The ultimate handbook

or anyone else on whom you rely that you have clear, attainable objectives.

David Jenkins is an accountant turned vineyard owner. He had been working in Italy for nine years, earning £70,000, owning a beautiful home and three cars, and taking seven weeks' holiday a year. But it had become a lucrative treadmill. He married Paula in 1990 and, when their first child, Alexander, was born in 1992 they decided they had to get out. They settled on owning a vineyard in England quite by chance.

I was working as an auditor for a firm of chartered accountants. Italy hadn't had audited accounts until the late seventies and a lot of ex-pats went out. I liked the life and stayed, going to work for one of my clients, a washing machine company, and then an American multinational.

We lived in the country near Turin in a lovely house set in the hills, but I was working 15-hour days, and weekends too. I thought I'd have a heart attack sooner or later. I know Paula felt desperately isolated at home all day.

When I came home I was exhausted and didn't want to do anything. Work left no time for anything else. At home I was just recovering from work. It was hard for Paula integrating, especially with a young child.

I decided to resign and move back to England. I quit in April 1994 and said I'd stay until the end of the year to give me time to look around for something else. I knew the economic climate was not the best; it was a tough time to look for a job. A lot of chartered accountants in the UK had been made redundant. There were 500 people chasing every job and I'd had no UK experience for 15 years. I didn't get a single interview.

Then we saw an advert in the Daily Telegraph *for St Anne's Vineyard, which was for sale near Newent in Gloucestershire. We went to take a look. The idea of a vineyard came out of the blue, but it immediately appealed. In my spare time in Italy I had planted all sorts of vines on the 300 square metres of hills that I had. Unfortunately I didn't get much time to sample the wines.*

We didn't buy the vineyard to make our fortune. I was looking for something that would pay the bills, but not being able to get a job I was looking for any-thing that sounded interesting. We didn't want to live within the M25 or anything like that, the south did not appeal at all.

As soon as we saw the vineyard we fell in love with it. I like to think that I didn't set out to find a vineyard – it found me! And it matched my aspirations. We bought the house and four acres of land lock stock and barrel for £190,900. We had money from the sale of our house in Italy, but had to borrow £90,000 from the bank. The original owner said he'd give me a hand over the first year. He was a very, very good winemaker, so that clinched it.

We moved in in January 1995, when Paula was five months pregnant with our second son, Christopher. It was a complete change. The only relevant experience apart from dabbling in wine in Italy was that I was a keen amateur gardener. But this was 2,500 vines which could produce 9,000 bottles in a good year.

I was extremely busy the first six months. I had all the bottling and all the pruning to do, which you'd nor-mally start November time. I hardly drew breath, it was a seven-day-a-week, 12-hour-a-day job. By June I just about managed to get on top of it.

I had to set up the house and everything and I knew nothing about wine. You wake up some mornings thinking 'Oh my God, what have I done?' but you just have to get up, go out and get on with it.

The first month we opened was January 1996, and we took only £550 in the shop – which Paula runs – and the interest on the loans was £1,000. But it improved each month. In the first April we took £3,000 which met our target, and we haven't looked back.

It's difficult to make good wine. You need to know a certain amount about it and you never stop learning. There are lots of different theories, you have to find the best for your situation. Last summer should have been great but we had a late frost in April and we had a very low harvest. We only had 25 per cent of the wine we would normally have. But the quality was good.

You don't make your fortune making wine in England. We also sell a lot of fruit wines which bail us out. We are better known for them than grape wine. We do everything – 20 different varieties from pears and apples through to all the currants, loganberry, tayberry, all sorts of weird and wonderful fruit.

There are still pressures but they are different ones. They are your own, rather than somebody else saying you have to do this or that by a certain date. Most things you can put off to the next day if you really want to. The winter is wine-making and pruning the vines, the summer is looking after them, and the autumn is harvesting.

I've also bought another plot of land so I've almost doubled my capacity to grow grapes and I'm planting that up at the moment. You don't get your money back for about four years from when the first grapes appear. It is all money and effort at the start, you get your

Taking Care of Business

rewards down the line. Financially it's not that brilliant at the moment.

The big plus is that I see the family so much more. We are on a quiet country road – too quiet from a sales point of view – but great for the kids. They are very safe here. We are surrounded by woods, it is a big daffodil area, a very nice part of the world.

At the moment I do everything, but I might get somebody in to help me part-time. At present I even do the harvest myself.

I've no regrets. I certainly don't miss the stress of the job. What I did is very risky – a leap into the unknown. You need a strong will to succeed and a certain amount of financial backing initially.

Here, my office is 10 yards from my house and there is no commuting. I remember when we first arrived we stopped the car and I said: 'Listen.' All you could hear was bird song. I thought, 'Right, this is what I need after all the stress.' I still feel the same.

Emma Louise Salter did a degree in anthropology then trained as a chef. She worked in Bibendum and Langans Brasserie among others until she reached a point where she never wanted to cook again. She went into restaurant PR but was still unhappy. The stresses built up until she realised that she had not had a period for two years and decided she had to sort herself out.

She had tried vacuflexology as a patient. The treatment is a system of relieving discomfort and pain which combines the techniques of reflexology and needle-free acupuncture.

Vacuflexology worked so well for me that I decided to study as a vacuflexology practitioner, which took

18 months. Now I have my own practice based in a mews house close to Paddington Station in London.

My youngest patient is a boy of two whose eczema was so bad that his skin was supurating, but now I have virtually cleared it. Another success was a woman who had been trying for a baby for seven years. She came to me to get as healthy as possible before embarking on IVF treatment. After three sessions she cancelled everything – she was expecting twins.

I have taken a drop in income doing this, but it is incredibly rewarding just seeing the variety of people who come and of course helping them to get better.

The treatment works in two stages. The first uses felt boots which you put on the patient's feet. The air is sucked out of them to create a vacuum around both feet. The second uses suction pads rather than needles to stimulate the acupuncture meridians.

Stage one simultaneously works every reflex point on the soles of the feet and can last from 5 to 20 minutes. It is a painless way to work the reflex points, and it also gives a deeper treatment than conventional reflexology.

After the boots are removed I look at the soles of the feet to see if any area has turned a different colour. This is a sign of blockages or toxic build-up and alerts me to what areas may need more work. In Stage two all the acupuncture meridians are worked on to restore the body's electrical balance, aid relaxation and promote healing.

The therapy works on the central nervous system, and detoxifies the body. I treat asthma, insomnia, menstrual pains, infertility and prostate problems, migraine, depression, allergies, digestive problems, sluggish circulation, rheumatoid arthritis and stiff joints, stress and many other complaints.

When you start up a business you have got to sell yourself. In an office you are at the centre of things. I'm sitting here alone in a mews house and if the phone doesn't ring I am out of business. You have got to create your own buzz.

My quality of life is so much better now. Working in a kitchen it is manic. People there can be so chauvinistic. I was usually the only woman in a kitchen. But it doesn't have to be so unpleasant. I worked in San Francisco and there they are calm, and the cooking is every bit as good.

You need quite a lot of support when you change careers in the way I did. For one thing the training was very intense. It is not a lark. I had to do it at weekends while I was holding down another job. And then there is the hard slog of building up the business.

A lot of alternative medicine people think it's easy to get patients, but if one is being honest about it it is a long slog. It takes probably five years to build up a full practice. I've only been doing it for a year and a bit.

One of the most depressing things is when you sit and the phone goes several times and every time it is another patient cancelling a session.

If you are an orthodox doctor you go to a practice and when another doctor retires or passes away you buy his patient list. You can't really do that in alternative medicine.

When I was training I gave up PR and just did odd jobs. For a while I worked as a receptionist in a private doctor's. I thought 'Great, I'll be able to get some patients here.' But it didn't work out. Some practices have alternative medicine as part of the practice, but

The ultimate handbook

not there. I have a couple of friends now who are doctors and sometimes they send patients.

It costs about £5,000 to train. The vacuflexology machine costs about £2,500. It is a lot of money to find at the beginning.

If I'd have been told all that it would entail at the outset I am not sure if I would have gone in for it. It is expensive to train and after you train it's not like you are going to have 18 patients a day.

You build up from a base of nothing. Of the seven people I trained with I think I am practically the only one still practising.

When I decided to make the break I wasn't sure I should. I thought I loved restaurant PR, but everyone around me was saying what a nightmare I was to be with, they could see far better than I could. They were saying give it up, give it up, give it up.

The eighties were quite a difficult decade to be in. Because people around you were doing so well so quickly, and supposedly making a fortune, it was very easy to get caught up into thinking 'My God, if you haven't succeeded in three years you have got to change and do something else.' Which is very dangerous.

People live a lie. I'm quite an honest person and it is terribly easy to believe people when you sit at dinner and they say they are doing terribly well. But it can all be a bit of an illusion.

In the nineties people are more realistic, options are fewer and people have to work for things – which must be right. My parents' generation worked at something – maybe they didn't enjoy it but over 30–40 years they stuck at it and developed a skill.

If you are starting up a business you have to have that doggedness and dedication.

Pat and Tony Brown gave up their jobs as a teacher and a manager of a plant-hire firm respectively, sold their house in Essex and moved to Wales in 1988. They bought a dilapidated old farmhouse at Pant-teg, Llanfair Clydogau, Lampeter, for £59,000 and set about renovating it. Pat had planned to return to teaching, and Tony would do building work, at which he was experienced. But Pat found only Welsh-speaking teachers were required locally, so Tony kept them going with occasional building jobs. Friends who visited said their 19th-century home, with its four acres of land hugging the lower slopes of the Cambrian mountains, was so beautiful, and their hospitality so warm, that they should open a bed-and-breakfast hotel. They did, and it has been a great success.

In Essex both Tony and I were very busy and we seemed to be working harder and harder just to sustain the mortgage. We had no time to ourselves. One day we took stock and decided to look at an alternative way of life.

We came across Lampeter, liked the town and began searching for a home. Within five minutes of seeing Pant-teg we had decided to buy it, despite the fact it was dingy and needed a lot of work doing to it. To us it seemed magical.

The weather was awful the day we arrived. The furniture van couldn't get down the lane and we had to transfer all our belongings to a smaller van in the rain. It was an absolute nightmare.

Then all of our friends started coming, told us what a fantastic place we had, and sent their friends. We always seemed to have a house full of people. It was Tony who said we ought to earn our living by providing holiday accommodation.

It cost between £25,000 and £30,000 to convert the place, but it would have been a lot more if Tony had not been able to undertake most of the work himself. Two bathrooms were added and a small barn was converted into an en-suite bedroom and linked to the farmhouse by means of a conservatory area where visitors eat. We completely re-roofed the property, the walls were raised and a guest lounge created upstairs. Outside a borehole was sunk to provide a constant supply of fresh spring-water.

Our final project was the renovation of a former pottery behind the main house, which we've turned into a self-catering unit for six people.

Living here you have to be content with our own company. It can be quite isolated. You have to take pleasure in country life. But we wouldn't swap it for anything. Tony still does some building work, and every summer he helps the local farmers to catch and shear their sheep. I use some of the wool to make rugs, hats and other things.

It is ironic. When we started out, failure was the big worry. We never thought about the problems of success. But recently the business has become so successful that it has been affecting our quality of life. To cut down on work we have stopped offering meals in the summer and vowed not to let work take over our lives again.

Work creeps up on you. We found we were getting less time that we wanted for ourselves, and for enjoying the countryside. But we don't regret coming here for one moment.

DECISIONS

So, do you want to start your own business? Are you cut out for the role of self-employed businessperson?

To help you decide, work on a business plan. Answer the questions posed in this chapter about your plans. And also look at the questions on page 107 which relate to you as a person, and your suitability to run a business.

How do your plans – and you – shape up under that scrutiny?

CHAPTER SEVEN

Voluntary Action

I HAVE a confession to make. I believe downshifting can make the world a better place. Not just for the downshifter, but for everyone.

The reasoning is simple. When you downshift you have more time both for yourself and, if you so choose, to do things for others. As mentioned in Chapter 4, downshifters are seeking a healthy balance between paid work, family commitments, hobbies, voluntary work and other interests.

For some downshifters, of course, the main aim in changing their lives is so they can devote themselves to doing good works. A couple of such people are featured in the case studies in this chapter.

But every downshifter can help in some way. As many downshifters developed highly valued skills in their previous employment, it follows that many of them have talents which they may now, if they wish, offer for free to those who could not normally afford them.

Any of the professions – accountants, lawyers, public relations executives, teachers, army officers, civil servants and the rest – can bring huge benefits to any number of voluntary bodies.

Very often, however, it is simply your time rather than any particular skill that is of value to a charity, voluntary body or community organisation. These days, for example, state infant and junior schools are often desperate for parent helpers to lighten the load of teachers struggling with large class sizes and the demands of the national curriculum. Many downshifters I have spoken to spend a morning or afternoon a week helping out at the local school.

Many others help run youth organisations such as the Brownies, Cubs, Guides and Scouts. Others organise youth clubs.

The modern demands of work have meant that the very people who were once the backbone of social and community organisations now have no time in which to lend their help and support. There is, for instance, a shortage of school governors. Recently the Department of Education launched a £445,000 campaign to attract 60,000 new ones.

Downshifters are ideally situated to take on a role such as that of school governor. Others may become parish, town or district councillors, or even magistrates. In doing so they help strengthen the fabric of their local community.

Many of our most important local institutions have always relied upon the committed volunteer. Downshifters can fill these roles in a way that many who are still in full-time work simply cannot anymore.

In 1989, then-Prime Minister Margaret Thatcher said famously: 'There is no such thing as Society. There are individual men and women, and there are families.' Downshifting is – partly – about refuting this statement. Downshifters believe that society matters and that, without it, we have mere selfishness. A sense of community, of society, is one of the driving forces behind the actions of many downshifters, and is to be applauded.

Part-time voluntary work is not the whole story. Some downshifters go the whole hog – giving up the vast bulk of their time to voluntary work. Others switch to work that pays less but is more socially useful, in which they can help others, not just themselves.

Kevin Vickers switched to part-time work for the National Westminster Bank in order to become an ordained minister at his local church.

Karen Gorbett gave up her highly-paid career as a recruitment consultant and became a probation officer.

Peter Whitaker gave up his job as an academic in order to found and run a one-man mountain rescue service.

John Martyn quit his job in the City to do voluntary work for the homeless.

Exactly what you volunteer for is, of course, a very personal decision influenced by all sorts of unique factors, and will often involve work in your local community. But it is worth considering spreading your net a little wider. Experienced people are desperately needed by charities for all sorts of work in Great Britain and abroad. And if you don't know where to begin as a volunteer, there are various oganisations ready to help steer you in the right direction.

For example, there is an umbrella organisation called the Volunteer Centre UK which is the national development agency for volunteering. It believes that volunteering is a distinctive and important aspect of life in the United Kingdom – 'A powerful and abiding force for change for both those who volunteer and the wider community.'

The centre is a sort of clearing house, matching organisations that want volunteers with those who wish to help and have particular skills to offer. It has an extensive library and database with information on local volunteering opportunities and data provided by organisations ranging from Barnados and the Community Development Foundation to the National Youth Agency, The Joseph Rowntree Trust and the British Library of Development Studies. It publishes information about volunteering in your local area, in the UK generally and overseas, and material on specific areas of voluntary work such as working with children or the environment.

Simply by providing the Volunteer Centre with your postcode, they will send you a list of organisations in your locality which accept volunteers. They also run a network of local Volunteer Bureaux, which act as 'job shops' for those who are interested in volunteering but who are unsure which organisation could best do with their help.

You might want to work with animals, in a charity shop, with the disabled, with the elderly, with those with learning difficulties or with the young, in a museum, a nature reserve or a country park. Whatever your preferred area, the Volunteer Centre can tell you what opportunities are available so you are fully informed before you step forward with your offer of help.

But the Volunteer Centre is by no means the only port of call open to you.

Voluntary Service Overseas, or VSO, used to be solely about young people travelling to impossible places. But that is no longer the case. Now, volunteers at the upper end of the age scale are putting their hard-earned skills and knowledge to new use.

Through an arm of an organisation called British Executive Service Overseas (BESO), 800 people a year are sent to tackle complex problems all over the world. Founded in 1978, BESO recycles the skills of mature volunteers to the developing world and the former Soviet bloc.

The organisation finds that, with retirement ages falling and increasing numbers of people opting out of their careers when they still have plenty of years and energy left, there are increasing numbers of energetic former executives who would like nothing more than to jump on a plane and tackle a new challenge. BESO has the people with the professional skills to tackle all manner of problems, from former senior customs officers who can assist a rag-tag force in a third world country struggling to thwart highly organised and well-equipped smugglers, to broadcasters who can launch a TV station.

The guiding principle behind BESO is that people are of more value than financial aid to developing countries. Volunteers go abroad as trainers or advisers on assignments that can last for anything from two weeks to six months. When they go, the expectation is, they will leave behind organisations in a position to run their own affairs, and at a fraction of the cost of bringing in paid, professional consultants.

Many of BESO's volunteers are classic downshifters. They told me, for example, about one 49-year-old volunteer called Richard Tufnell. Richard was an estate agent in Hampshire before quitting the rat race and escaping to Scotland, where he and his wife bought a farmhouse with three-quarters of a mile of crumbling dry-stone walls. He learned the skills required to renovate the walls.

Those skills came in extremely useful when the Lutheran Development Service in Swaziland approached BESO to request a trainer who could teach local people to convert the abundance of loose rocks found locally into walls to contain livestock and delineate fields. Mr Tufnell was sent over. The first problem he hit was that, while rocks for stone-walling in Britain come in various shapes and sizes which can be skilfully fitted together, the rocks in Swaziland were all uniformly grapefruit-sized and round. Making them hold together without mortar was hugely problematic.

On a previous visit to Africa, however, Richard had discovered that in the bush of Zimbabwe, material from termite hills was used as makeshift mortar. He taught the people he was advising to do the same. As a result, he was able to build a causeway across a river which was normally impassable for three months of the year. Now remote villages are accessible all year round, which means people can travel for work or schooling.

With volunteering, every little helps. And, in total, voluntary work is very valuable indeed. The Volunteer Centre says that the economic value of voluntary work in Great Britain is in the region of £41 billion a year. That is, certainly, well below the value of service industries, at £330 billion per year, and manufacturing at £107 billion, but is comfortably above the construction industry (£36 billion), and way above agriculture (£7 billion).

Each year in the UK, over 20 million people volunteer, providing a service which, in the words of the Voluntary Centre, is above price. 'Any attempt to replace it with paid work,' the organisation says, 'would change its very nature, replacing a relationship based on social responsibility and mutual aid with one based on financial gain.'

No such thing as society? Ask those 20 million volunteers or, indeed, the four people whose case studies are outlined below.

Kevin Vickers, 35, is an assistant manager and small business adviser for NatWest who has reduced his hours to 15 a week in order to become a minister involved in pastoral care and teaching at the Gladstone Mission Evangelical Church in Mitcham, Surrey.

I've been going to my church ever since I was a boy. I was asked to become an elder when I was 30. As

I was taking on more responsibility I felt there was a need to get fully involved. While working for the bank I was always interested in teaching and preaching the bible, so I started to do some courses while I was at work. I went to Spurgeons Bible College, which is a Baptist college, and did some courses there while working full-time. As I took on more responsibility at the church – I was working with the youth, organising small group bible studies and that sort of thing – I realised that there needed to be somebody around during the day.

In our church we don't have a sole, full-time minister as such. There are three elders who fulfil all those functions between them. But we all had full-time day jobs. So I put it to the church about spending more time around the church. I spoke to the bank, too.

The bank was ever so positive. When I first went to them I had intended giving in my notice and going to bible college full-time. But the person in the regional office whom I spoke to suggested keeping it off the record for the time being, while I completed my negotiations with the college and worked out the financial situation. It was the bank that suggested I go part-time. They were introducing a particular scheme at the time called the Career Change Programme and I was the first assistant manager to be accepted. I got a lump sum that helped pay college fees as well.

I talked to my wife Jane and our three young children – Samuel (8), Rachel (7) and Jonathan (6) – we discussed all the implications. We assumed it would mean a big reduction in lifestyle and we were prepared for that. My wife doesn't work, other than the odd cleaning job now and again. But that hasn't really come about. We have found that, with the bank salary and *donations that we get from the church, we have managed to make ends meet.*

I'd like to think I am doing more good now, but whatever you are doing you should do to the best of your ability – as a Christian I believe that – so that you get satisfaction out of whatever you are doing. My roles are so varied that I get huge satisfaction out of both. The days at the bank tend to be Monday and Friday. They are fairly stable, I tend to know what I will be doing. But the other three days are incredibly varied. I could be taking a funeral or doing a school assembly or running a baptismal class or marriage preparation classes – all sorts of things.

No two weeks are the same. It is a very fulfilling way of life. Both jobs involve working with people and it has shown me more than anything that it is people who matter.

Many people who work full-time have a lot to offer their communities, if only they could free up enough of their time to do so. The key is getting the balance right, which is not an easy thing to do. But if I manage my time correctly then everyone benefits. My family see more of me, I work from home quite a bit. I can pick the children up from school and take them to their after-school clubs.

As a Christian minister, the ability to relate to people who are holding down a job in the real world is very important. Knowing the same stresses and hassles as those in the congregation enhances what I preach about on Sunday.

Karen Gorbett lives in southeast London. She switched from a career with an information technology recruitment company to train to be a probation officer.

I started out in a sales capacity, and there were monthly or quarterly sales targets to achieve. You were only as good as your last sale and what you earned depended on what you brought in. There was the opportunity to make a lot of money. I had the company Golf GTi and so on. Then I moved into a project management position where I was only dealing with a couple of accounts, taking on that company's recruitment. I stuck it for three years and I was the longest-serving member of staff.

I found a hideous commercial mentality at the company. There was no paid overtime and it didn't matter at what time you left at night, if you arrived at one minute past nine the next day you were humiliated publicly, yelled at. People's opinion of you depended on how much money you raked in in sales.

I was unhappy for a long time, but I didn't have a professional vocation. I'd done A levels, gone to college and had a good basic education but it was totally dispensable at the end of the day. My future was dictated by the economic climate and the needs of the company for my services. So no matter what hours or effort I was putting in I could be got rid of.

There was stress, humiliation and racial and sexual discrimination on a daily basis. I realised that, staying in that work, my destiny was not in my hands. But I did not have the time to look around and think about what to do.

Before I could get things sorted out and leave they sacked me because they wanted me back in sales and I refused. I was on holiday and got a letter at home and was made redundant on basic statutory terms.

I went into a panic. I had a mortgage. But I had typing skills I'd picked up from using computers so

Voluntary Action

I became a temp. It was then I had a chance to think about what I should be doing long term. I took career counselling and decided I wanted to be a probation officer. I decided on this career by looking at the skills I had which were transferable. I had always worked with people, always made assessments of them, and had had to get to know them quite quickly.

I knew social work would not be quite right, and I did not want to work with children. There was PR but that was back in the commercial world and I couldn't hack that again.

In an ideal world I would have wanted to be a solicitor but I did not have the money to study for that.

I settled on becoming a probation officer. I had to support myself, living on my own with a mortgage. To get on the course you have to do voluntary work and to have got paid work of a similar nature. So while still temping I did Saturday voluntary work and kept my eyes open for a job. I got one in a bail hostel. I did that for a year and then applied for social work training, and now I'm a probation officer.

I am much happier. The job I do now is worthwhile. I can help people, I can make a positive difference in their lives. I can be me, I've stopped trying to be dynamic, stopped sacrificing my principles. Then I was being asked to do underhand things to get a sale and make a profit, now there are not those commercial pressures.

Now people accept me for what and who I am. Before I was criticised for not being tough enough. I can dress as I choose, I don't need the face full of make-up and the power dressing.

I now believe that I am doing good with the work that I do. I know that I may not see a direct result from my efforts with a person while I am working with them, but that input may work down the line. It is not a wasted effort. And the service is not just to the clients, it is to the court and the community.

I earn less now than I did six years ago, but it's not difficult to cope. I just adapted.

I hated the other job, I hated what I was becoming. I would never go back, not if they offered me twice the salary.

Peter Whitaker, 56, spent most of his working life as a lecturer in reprographics at the Cardiff Institute. He is divorced with three grown-up children. In 1984 he moved to live alone in a remote house in the Brecon Beacons. Within four days people in difficulties began knocking at his door asking for help, and he has been involved in over 900 rescues over the years.

I had been teaching for about 20 years when, at the end of one term, I realised I was sick of it and I simply didn't go back.

The rescue service, which I call the Mountain Help Centre, started by accident. I had come to live in the only house for miles around. The first people I helped were the army. Soldiers on an exercise knocked on the door at half-eleven at night, at half-one and again at half-three. We were in the thick of a blizzard and they were asking 'Can you tell us where we are?'

I have helped everyone over the years. The map on my wall tells me I've done 942 call-outs in 10 years. I do one on average every two-and-a-half days. A couple of years ago four SAS men dropped in, two of them suffering from hypothermia. I forced a mug of hot tea into one man's frozen hands. As he gulped it down he murmured, 'Without you here I'd have died.'

They aren't all life-or-death incidents. Last week there was a £40,000 four-wheel-drive stuck in the mud, so I pulled it out and the driver gave me £20 and I nearly fainted. On average I probably make only a couple of pounds a week.

Why do I do it? I was driven to it, because I have the skills and because I have saved children's lives. And because it gives me a purpose in life. I am a very solitary person and I live a very unusual lifestyle. It is not for everybody, but I was prepared to give up everything. I used to live in a 14-room house and now I'm in a tiny little place. I am very poor but there is something very satisfying about helping people.

I never go away; I want to keep a permanent presence on the mountains. I act as a telephone point. I liaise with police and mountain rescue groups; I'm the first point of contact with people who are in trouble.

John Martyn, 53, resigned as the £220,000-a-year finance director of a multinational pet food manufacturer to join his wife at the Gateway charity for the homeless, which she founded in Oxford, and to become unpaid treasurer of a charitable concern linked with two local psychiatric hospitals. He told the *Daily Express*:

I don't want to be seen as holier than thou. I've made a great deal of money in my time. I have a full pension and a sideline as a non-executive director, so I'm in a very fortunate position. But increasingly over the years I have been drawn to charity work and I find myself in a position where I couldn't now simply put my feet up and do nothing. I'm determined to help those who are less privileged than I.

The ultimate handbook

Obviously some people are surprised at my decision. Working with less privileged people is not the most glamorous role. But I am thoroughly enjoying it and am delighted to be rolling up my sleeves for a worthy cause.

When I saw the work my wife was doing in Oxford I became very keen to get involved. Nowadays I act as a kind of minder when things go wrong between the people who come in and use the centre. Most people come in for a cup of tea and a quiet read of the paper. But there are plenty of fights that break out and someone has got to sort them out.

Of course, if someone had told me 20 years ago that this was the kind of work I would be doing I would have laughed. But I think it is a great way to put something back into the community.

DECISIONS

Decide what part of your life you will devote to voluntary work. Once you know how many hours a week you can spare, you can begin to look at the best way to spend that time. The organisations listed in the Resources chapter can help you take it from there.

CHAPTER EIGHT

Back to School

ONE OF the great pluses of downshifting is that it may give you the time and opportunity to study. What you study may, of necessity, be entirely practical. If you plan to open a business, you may be working towards qualifications which will enable you to succeed in that undertaking. If you are planning a career change you may be studying for additional qualifications which will help you to make that move. To that end you may study full-time at a university, or part-time via anything from the Open University to evening classes at your local college.

But you may well be studying for purely 'selfish' reasons – taking the degree you always wish you had taken in your youth, learning the language you have always wanted to master, tackling a new discipline simply to stretch your mind, or learning about a craft for the satisfaction of being able to create something you could not have created before.

Even if there is absolutely no need for study in your new, downshifted life, I would urge you to give over part of your new portfolio lifestyle to study. It might be simply two hours a week at evening school, but it will add to the richness of your new life. It will give you time to yourself, and time to develop a new skill. To take up an exciting new challenge is life-enhancing, and it may lead to greater things.

Every teacher of evening classes has a favourite tale of great achievement, whether it is about the woman who came along to do flower arranging simply for the fun of it but who got hooked and now owns a flower shop, or the man who started off with conversational French, went on to do a degree in the language, and now runs a hotel in Normandy.

Here are five examples of downshifters who have slotted study into their new lives:

> Anneka Rice put her career as a television presenter on hold in order to study art, simply for the fun of it.
>
> Elaine Fyne was forced to give up dentistry after a severe road accident, and took ceramics classes as therapy. Now she has a pottery business.
>
> Laurence Walton was a successful shop manager, but had always had a chip on his shoulder about not having a degree. He took the plunge at 44 and is studying theology.
>
> Yvonne Smith, 36, studied for a BA part-time while working in a carpet factory; she is now a teacher.
>
> Gary Richardson took a career break from his banking job to do a Master of Business Administration degree.

There have been concerted attempts at Government level to instil in the population at large a vision of learning as not merely something for the young but a pursuit that should continue throughout life.

The logic of this is undeniable, and will be easily grasped by any downshifter. They know better than anybody about the impacts that the changing nature of work are having. Indeed, they are often downshifting because of these changes.

The ultimate handbook

Gillian Shepherd, former Secretary of State for Education, has said:

Anyone who stands still while the world changes around them will soon find that the world has passed them by. We must face the reality that tastes change, products change and markets change. When that happens, jobs will change too.

Learning pays ... in today's world, skills, knowledge and adaptability are at a premium. Those who continue to learn and re-learn will be better paid and are far less likely to be unemployed.

As a mature student of whatever standing you will not be lonely. Each September well over a million Britons enrol in evening classes of some kind or another. Of these, 350,000 tap into local university resources, and 750,000 take courses at adult education centres. A third of undergraduates at British universities are now mature students, and every year around 30,000 'distance learners' enrol for the Open University, studying very largely at home with the help of television programmes, summer schools and – increasingly – the Internet.

Of course, not all these people are downshifters, but many are, and the wide range of facilities for adult education of whatever form give a huge amount of choice to the downshifter, and dovetail well with his or her new life.

The National Institute of Adult Continuing Education (NIACE) carries out regular surveys into adult education and those who take it, and their findings reveal that the sorts of courses which will appeal particularly to downshifters are very popular. Adult education follows trends, and in the nineties personal development is the big issue. The most popular courses are for people trying to improve or understand themselves and deal with the world of work. Courses to improve personal and professional skills are in great demand, especially those in computing and counselling.

NIACE says that opportunities to study vary around the country but that, in general, while opportunities to gain higher-level qualifications are booming, more basic courses have been hit by cuts in local authority budgets.

With universities and colleges offering courses in subjects covered traditionally by local authorities, there is a bewildering choice. Picking the right course for you can be complex, so the advice is to take soundings from as many sources as possible to avoid embarking on a course only to discover, halfway through, is not for you.

Let us take evening classes first. There are certainly thousands of courses to choose from, ranging from painting and pottery to Word for Windows and conversational French. There are courses in craft subjects such as woodwork and DIY central heating, gas appliance servicing, ragging, rolling and stencilling, decoy duck carving and saddlery. There are courses in hairdressing, manicure, designing lingerie; language courses specifically designed for relief aid workers, courses in massage, aromatherapy, weightlifting, boxing, bodybuilding and Scottish country dancing. You name it, someone, somewhere is running a course in it.

Typically, born-again pupils start with a non-vocational subject and refine their interests as they become more confident. They might come for a pottery class one year and end up doing a degree in sociology five years later.

They often have high ideals, and see the course they are embarking on as putting them on a fast-track to a new them.

For those who did not take part in further education in their youth, going back to school after many years away can be daunting. But it shouldn't be, because – as a mature student – your relationship with the tutor is very different to that which you endured as a pupil. At school, you start out in total ignorance of your subject and rely totally on your teacher to enlighten you, guide you through it and gradually shed light on the topic. But when you return to the classroom in later life, the relationship between pupil and teacher is a much more balanced one because of all the experience you have behind you.

But what if evening classes are not enough, or if the course you want to follow is not available within easy reach of your home?

Distance-learning courses could be the answer. They enable people to study at home under a tutor's guidance, and there is – again – plenty of choice. The Open College of the Arts (OCA), affiliated to the Open University and accredited by Thames Valley University, has more than 20,000 students on courses specialising in every area of creative art, from sculpture to garden design.

The Association of British Correspondence Colleges (ABCC) covers hundreds of subjects, including GCSE, A-level, professional qualifications and vocational courses. Courses are also available on computer disk, with colleges using e-mail or fax for communication with students.

But perhaps you wish to study full-time for a degree? Mature students are now a sizable minority of undergraduates at UK universities and colleges. Many of them feel they missed out at school and are keen to make up for lost time. They are grasping at a second chance.

Going to university will no doubt be far more daunting than an evening class ever could be, but a recent Plymouth University study found that mature students do better than school-leavers, even if they have few or even no academic qualifications. Statistics showed that students aged over 25 without A-levels gained better degrees in all subjects.

Most seats of learning will consider older applicants who do not have the standard qualifications required for a course. They often offer places, after an interview, on the basis of motivation and potential. An alternative is an Access course, providing the work skills and knowledge students need for higher education.

For those who do not want to give up work while they gain their degree, home study courses are the simplest option. The most popular provider of these being the Open University.

The OU is the acknowledged leader in distance learning. It teaches by radio and television programmes, linked with correspondence courses, regular tutorials near the student's home and short-term residential schools. For the OU student, tutorial, counselling and support services are organised by the 13 regional centres which together are responsible for about 250 local study centres throughout the UK, with 5,500 part-time tuition and counselling staff.

Betty Boothroyd, speaker of the House of Commons and chancellor of the OU since 1994, has said: 'The OU occupies a unique place in the academic world and in our national life. It offers the opportunity for higher education and thus for self-fulfilment to thousands of men and women of all ages and backgrounds who could not otherwise enjoy this privilege.'

Well over two million have studied with the university. Created by Harold Wilson in 1969, it was founded on the principle that it was to be an independent university and open to all. There are no qualifications required of undergraduates. Its students are formidable people who have gained their degrees over an average of six years of hard slog, usually while holding down a full-time job.

The OU has some distinguished graduates. Robert Waters from St Andrews, Fife, manages Britain's fleet of 150 Tornado aircraft. He left school, where sport dominated his life, without any qualifications and joined the RAF. There his football coach suggested he got some O-levels. The learning bug bit and he went on to do a vocational qualification before studying with the OU. He believes that the BSc he has gained at the OU will help him to get a job when he leaves the RAF.

Graham Thomas of Oakham, Rutland, is one of Britain's few black police chief inspectors. He joined the force as a cadet aged 16, and later took the internal police examinations to become a sergeant and then an inspector. But he felt that, without a degree, he was losing out to policemen with academic qualifications. The OU degree enabled him to compete as an equal.

Increasingly, computer technology will be the key to adult education. By 2004 the Open University will expect its students to have access to a personal computer with a CD-ROM drive and modem. Students are eager for such innovation, it seems. When the OU's first course on the Internet was launched, 60 students from 18 countries signed up within three days of the course being listed on the Internet.

The fastest-growing arm of the OU is the Open Business School. Founded in 1983, it now has 20,000 students scattered across Europe, and its lecturers travel from Edinburgh to Moscow to give tutorials. It offers a number of management programmes, but the Master of Business Administration is its flagship.

Anyone who enrols on a course, whether an evening class in flower arranging or a degree in astrophysics, is making an act of faith. They see themselves as a different, better person by the end of it – and such dreams go to the heart of the philosophy behind downshifting.

Anneka Rice has had a successful, 15-year career as a television presenter on programmes including *Treasure Hunt* and *Challenge Anneka*, where she performed seemingly impossible charitable feats against the clock. She decided at the age of 33 to take a year away from the limelight to study art on a pre-foundation course at the Chelsea College of Art.

I've always wanted to be a painter, it's what I started out doing. I planned for three years to take some time off. I wanted a year off on my own, just to do my own thing.

Painting has always been my private passion, I just hadn't had the time to take up a paintbrush in years, so I decided I had to be ruthless and say to the BBC 'I'm sorry, I'm going to resign and cut everything else out.' Painting is not something you can muck about with because it is so intensive.

It's also regenerative, it's marvellous to do something you love, however hard. It can be used as therapy. It can be a healing process.

It's good to do different things at different times in your life. I'm lucky enough to be able to choose not to work for a while, having worked terribly hard for 15 years. It's time for a respite. It gives me a great sense of freedom, having been hemmed in by contracts and deadlines all that time. My children are delighted with what I'm doing now, they love it. They think it's funny that we all go off to our classes during the day and compare notes over tea when we come home.

It's everyone's dream, to take a sabbatical, to do what they want, but most people can't because they are tied into a job and need the money and can't take time out. Everyone has a desire to fulfil their creativity, but if you are working in a bank all day you can't afford, or you don't dare, to take time to do it.

Elaine Fyne, 44, had to give up her career as a dentist in 1992 after a serious road accident left her with multiple

The ultimate handbook

fractures and severe memory loss. To occupy herself, she took up pottery. She passed a two-year City and Guilds course in ceramics and is about to open her own pottery business.

Having to give up the career that I loved was a terrible blow. I felt my whole life had been destroyed in one fell swoop. I had never married or had children because my career always took precedence over everything else in my life.

I was deeply depressed when the severity of my injuries sank in. I have no idea how the accident happened, and nor does anybody else. I was found beside the road, where I had been knocked from my bike by a hit-and-run driver. Having no one to blame made me very bitter.

The process of recovery was a long one. I had no idea what to do with myself or what my other gifts might be. Ceramics had been an interest at school, but I had never studied the subject seriously. But, faced with the desperate need to do something with my time, I signed up for a ceramics evening class. Fortunately I had very good insurance which meant I had just about enough to live on.

As I recovered from my injuries I found myself enjoying making pots and other things more and more. I began to do other things, painting designs on plates and tiles, and making models of rocking horses and other things. My flat began to fill up with these things, and friends started to admire them. They made perfect birthday and Christmas presents and gradually quite a wide circle of people had seen my work and complimented me on it.

The rocking horses seemed particularly popular, and I began to be given commissions for them. People would have me put a child's name on them, say, and would give them as Christening presents or whatever.

It finally dawned on me that there might be a wider market for what I was making, so I did some research and started placing small ads in appropriate magazines, and attending craft fairs.

The orders started as a trickle, but in the past year have snowballed. I took out a small bank loan and rented premises. I now have as much work as I can handle and am about to take on an apprentice.

That evening class has really been exactly the catalyst I needed. It sounds corny, but it has opened up a new life for me, when I had feared there was nothing left to look forward to.

Laurence Walton gave up a successful career in retail management to pursue a degree in theology.

It was my 44th birthday when I came home to my wife and told her that I could not stand it any longer at work. As the manager of a high street store I had done well in my career, but I just could not see my career developing in the present economic climate. What's more, the work had become meaningless. I had always wished I had taken a degree, and knew that if I was to do so I had to act right then.

Fortunately my wife was very understanding. She had taken several years off from work – she is a cashier in a bank – while our daughters were growing up. They have now both left home, one is married and the other is at university. We had been able to bring our mortgage down by a half thanks to a small inheritance I came into, and so, financially, it was feasible for us to exist on one salary.

The ultimate handbook

I had always had a chip on my shoulder about not having a degree. I failed my A-levels because I preferred playing rugby and all the drinking and socialising associated with the sport to studying. No matter how well work went, I still felt like a failure. I tried to rationalise it and tell myself that whether or not I had a degree was irrelevant to the kind of person I was – to my worth – but it was no good.

Theology was something that had never really been a concern of mine, to be honest. But when I decided to do a degree I thought there was no need to do anything practical. I was not studying to get a better job, but for the pure intellectual pleasure of studying.

I was terribly worried about how I would cope with writing essays, but I discovered that I loved studying and could hold my own against the younger students. This was definitely the right age and stage of life for me to return to education. I was far too busy having a good time when I was young to take advantage of what was on offer. I am halfway through the course at present and I have no idea what I will do at the end of it. But that is not the point. It's the journey I am enjoying; I am not hurrying to reach any particular destination.

Yvonne Smith, 36, left school without qualifications and became a spinner in a carpet factory. She studied for a BA part-time with the Open University and is now a teacher.

I had no intention of studying, but one day I was off sick from work and could not sleep. I was downstairs at some ungodly hour and I turned on the TV. There was an Open University programme on, part of an English Literature course and the lecturer was talking about Shakespeare's King Lear. *I have no idea why but I got hooked. I decided there and then that I would do a degree myself. I had always loved reading, but left school at 16 and had really never progressed beyond modern novels. The English Literature degree was fantastic. I found it great to get home from work with my brain numb and open a book and suddenly feel rejuvenated. I found I got a second wind at night when I was studying.*

As I studied for the degree I began to wonder if there was anything I could do with it. I took careers guidance and the subject of teaching came up. With the OU degree I won a place on a post-graduate teacher training course, and I was lucky enough to get a job the following September. I'm not using my degree directly – I teach reception in an infants school, but without it I would never have got this new career. The Open University got me out of the factory, and I will always be grateful for that.

Gary Richardson took a career break at the age of 28 from the NatWest bank in Luton, where he looks after a portfolio of corporate clients, to study full-time for an MBA at Cranfield.

I had been with the bank for four years, ever since I graduated. My first degree is in business administration, and I wanted badly to continue my studies. I knew an MBA would probably help my employment prospects, and so I was planning to resign to go back to studying. But then someone suggested I apply for the employment breaks scheme. I had not thought of it because it is usually used by women taking time off to start or raise a family.

But I applied and was accepted, which meant I did not have to leave my job to study. I did have to take a

*year without pay, and there was no guarantee of a job
at the end of it, but at least it meant I did not have to
totally burn my bridges.*

*I was able to do it because I have no commitments
at present, and knew that if I didn't do it now I might
never get round to it.*

*I thought it was good for me to take a year out in
any case. It gave me the chance to look around at what
other employers there might be and, although I never
actually got seriously tempted to work for someone
else, it did at least mean I had weighed up the other
options. There is no such thing as a job for life these
days. In fact, the company actively encourages you to
keep an open mind.*

*As it turns out, I have returned to similar work.
I look after a portfolio of corporate clients in the range
of £1 million plus turnover, the medium-sized companies, but I won't be doing this for ever, and with my
new qualification I have increased my marketability,
should I decide to make a move.*

DECISIONS

How important is further education to your downshifting
plans? If it is essential that you study full-time there are vital
financial considerations to be taken into account. Are you
eligible for a grant?

What level of qualification do you need?

If you are interested in a new career, think about a short
course which will give you a taste of what you can expect,
before you decide to study the subject in depth.

When choosing a course, take your time. There is a bewildering amount of choice, and competition between suppliers
is fierce.

Talk to the tutors about the commitment needed. Make sure you can handle the hours. Is it too demanding? Get as much advice as possible. Talk to employers, colleagues, friends.

Will your employer help? Ask about help with fees. If the course of study that interests you is work-related, firms will often help.

CHAPTER NINE

Move It

MOVING house will form part of the plans of many down-shifters. There are several reasons for this.

The desire to swap the urban nightmare for the rural idyll is a dream that inspires a large proportion of those who are motivated by a desire to improve their quality of life.

Today, with the explosion in computer communications, it is possible for a growing number of people to carry out their work from home. And, increasingly, that home can be anywhere. The Henley Centre has calculated that 50 per cent of jobs in London could be done at least in part by workers using home computers. The Office of National Statistics says that 700,000 already do so. In the US, 12 million workers are based at home. As the rewards for employers are lower costs and higher productivity – teleworkers are more flexible and take less sick leave – this trend is likely to accelerate.

A move may be necessary for financial reasons. You may need a cheaper house and a smaller mortgage if you are to downshift successfully.

The considerations above may combine. A newfound freedom from sitting in an office all week may make your dream of living in the place you love above all others a reality.

And, if housing is cheaper there, you may be able to acquire the sort of house you always wanted into the bargain.

But a move from town to country may not be enough for you. You may wish to move abroad, to a country where the opportunities and the quality of life are better than you perceive them to be at home.

Or you may find that you do not need to move at all. You may decide that you love your home and the neighbourhood in which you live. You may decide that the roots you have put down – the friends you have made among your neighbours, the schools your children are attending, the simple reassurance of being in a place that you know and in which you feel at home, mean that working from your existing house is the perfect solution for you.

Here are five people for whom moving was an important part of the downshifting equation:

> Anthony Capstick and his wife, Katie, wanted to live in his native village in Lancashire. They were able to do so by starting a financial information company that could be based anywhere.
>
> Kevin Attfield works in London for half the week, and from home – on the Isle of Bute – for the rest.
>
> Alan Denbigh halved his £30,000 a year salary and gave up his company car in order to take a job which he could do from home.
>
> Jane Palmer faced redundancy as an architect in London, but found a job and success in Germany.
>
> Freelance journalist Alan Smith moved from London to rural Kent, then back to his old street in Ealing.

The vast majority of downshifters who want to move wish to swap the city for either a smaller town, a village, or the remote countryside. They are worried about rising urban

The ultimate handbook

crime, their children's safety and the general low quality of life. Often they remember the relative freedom they had as children and, despairing at the way their own offspring have to be shepherded everywhere and protected from the twin perils of traffic and strangers, wish to give them a real childhood.

Certainly, the benefits of country living are not hard to identify. Property prices will tend to be cheaper, for one thing, as long as you do not go for the super-fashionable parts of the Cotswolds, and you will probably have a large garden rather than a cramped patio. Schooling tends to be better, and the city dwellers who felt that their children had to be educated privately – and very expensively – while living in town will often be happy with the free state education available in the country.

There are other financial benefits too. Both household and car insurance will tend to be lower. Workers, from builders and repair men to cleaners and babysitters, will be cheaper, and the absence of expensive shops will mean less temptation to splash out.

But – and this is a big but – today's countryside does not offer the rural utopia that many of us fondly remember from 20, 30 or 40 years ago. As the urban world has changed, so has the rural. A vastly expanded road network means that the country is no longer cut off from the towns. Cuts in education and other state provision have hit rural areas just as hard as urban ones. There are some sobering statistics available which put the rural dream in perspective.

According to the Rural Development Commission, for example, fewer than half of all rural parishes have a school. Which means children have to be ferried there and back and, as more than half of all parishes with fewer than 100 residents have no bus service, that means parents must use their cars. Even if there is a bus to take the children to school, they will need transporting to their other activities, which will tend to happen either at school or in the nearest town. Friends are likely to be scattered, and children can often believe they have a life which is far less rich than the apparently dynamic one enjoyed by their town-dwelling peers.

Country roads are not as safe as they were, either, so parents who remember cycling happily around the lanes as children may not be happy to allow their own children to do so. The Royal Society for the Prevention of Accidents say 202 children were killed or seriously injured in non-built-up areas of England in 1994.

The other great fear, of molestation, is also a very real one. Because so many people are moving to the country – statistics show the population of cities like Liverpool falling while those of country towns like Huntingdon increase – the old-fashioned method of community protection from dangerous outsiders – everyone knowing everyone else – has broken down.

Things are not, interestingly, as bad abroad.

The Policy Studies Institute (PSI) carried out a survey in 1990 which looked at five different parts of England and compared the results with a similar survey conducted in the same English towns in 1971. It also compared the results with five comparable areas of Germany.

In 1971, 80 per cent of English seven- and eight-year-olds were allowed to travel to school on their own or with other children. By 1990 this figure had dropped to below 10 per cent. But, in Germany, 60 per cent of that age group still went to school unaccompanied, and 90 per cent came home alone at the end of the day.

The PSI asked parents about their fears: traffic danger was cited by 43 per cent, and the risk of molestation and assault by 21 per cent.

Simply, the countryside is no longer the great open playground that it was a generation ago. Intensive farming means many fields are drenched with potentially harmful pesticides and, in an increasingly litigious age, farmers may chase a child off their land because their insurance will not cover them should the child be injured.

There are also some areas in which costs are higher if you live in the countryside. Transport, for one. You will probably use your car more and, if you have to travel regularly to London, for instance, you will find rail fares high. It also costs more to maintain rambling country houses, and to heat them.

None of the above is intended to suggest that a better life cannot be had in the countryside, but rather to encourage anyone thinking of such a move to ensure that they really know exactly what life in the countryside is like.

It is not a move that you can make on a whim, or without careful planning – perhaps over a number of years. Ideally you should spend some time in the place you plan to move to. That includes, if you want to move to a spot where you have had idyllic summer holidays, seeing what it is like in the depths of winter. Don't go too far too soon. Going from the inner city to the back of beyond may be too much to take at one go. Try a village first.

Any rural estate agent has tales of the family who wanted a rural retreat in Cornwall or Devon, and even insisted on the true isolation of Dartmoor or Bodmin Moor, only to ask them to re-market their new home after a matter of months. Remember that, wherever you buy, you get what you pay for. That fantastic detached house in the middle of nowhere may be cheaper than the smaller house in the village because few can stand its isolation and loneliness.

The one essential for getting the most out of country life is to take part. Join in everything you can – help at the church bazaars and with the village cricket teams, use the local shops and other businesses. You won't be accepted if you don't take part.

Move It

If you are to work from home for the first time in your new country house, there are a whole raft of other things you need to get used to. Work needs to be kept separate, as much as possible, from your new home life.

Home working is not merely good for the individual, according to Sir Terence Conran. In his book *Terence Conran on Design* he argues that many urban problems have been created by the separation between home and work. He asserts that many of the problems faced by towns and cities are the legacy of previous working patterns. It is separating work from social life that has given us the dormitory village, the commuter town and the featureless suburb. And, in addition, it has given us town centres where the population disappears each evening, leaving eerie emptiness.

Mixed-use communities, says Sir Terence, are vital communities. They have shops, workplaces, schools and leisure facilities side by side. Homeworking, as it spreads, can be the catalyst which brings all this about.

Another catalyst has been the creation of telecottages. These are technology centres set up in anything from a village, a town, a suburb or a city centre, though they tend to be rural. A telecottage, says Ashley Dobbs of the Telecottaging Association, is a technology centre which any number of local people can share. This means that they do not have to have expensive computer and communications equipment of their own. They can come into the telecottage when they need such facilities and work at home when they do not.

As a builder, Mr Dobbs quickly grasped the importance of the concept when first introduced to it 10 years ago. He began building telecottages and televillages – often converting disused rural buildings into housing where there were dedicated facilities for homeworkers in each. He got large numbers of inquiries from would-be telecottagers and, when

The ultimate handbook

around 40 telecottages were in existence, decided to set up the Telecottaging Association in 1993.

He says:

I thought as a housebuilder that I should be building houses geared more to people working from home. I changed my company's name from Acorn Restorations to Acorn Tele-villages and built a telehamlet, eight houses round a very pleasant cobbled courtyard, with separate offices grouped together, in Hertfordshire. The beauty of it was that people had the benefit of having a separate office away from home with the advantage of not having to travel to work, but not being isolated from other people.

I went on to build the first true televillage at Crickhow-ell in Wales. Now I have put forward a proposal to build a televillage of 400 homes, all of them linked up by fibre-optics and local area networking.

Emigration has always had a strong lure for the British, and can be of great appeal to downshifters. Studies of people intending to leave Britain cite the desire for a healthier, cleaner, less stressed life as the main reasons for wanting to emigrate.

In a survey of 1,300 conducted by Outbound News-papers, which publishes five monthly magazines for potential leavers, 3 per cent sought a better lifestyle, 20 per cent said they were simply disillusioned with Britain. So overwhelming is the sense of disappointment in their homeland that 47 per cent said they would apply to emigrate to another country if their first choice turned them down.

Often they had carried out little research into life in the country they hoped to move to. Of those wishing to move to New Zealand, 56 per cent had never been there; over a third of those aiming to go to Australia and Canada had never visited.

Research compiled by the Office of Population Census-es and Surveys in London and the European Commission in Brussels suggests that emigration is running at its highest level for a decade. Around 150,000 native Britons are leaving each year, a rate which exceeds that of people moving to the UK from abroad.

The pattern of emigration has changed dramatically. For much of this century, Britons have gone where colonial ties took them: Australia, Canada and South Africa above all, and unskilled workers were as welcome as the highly qualified. But in the past 20 years there has been a change. Anyone without further education or technical skills will find it very difficult indeed. The skills which each country is seeking in would-be immigrants vary from year to year. In Canada, industrial mechanics and catering workers are twice as much in demand now as they were five years go, while the chances of an undertaker or computer programmer being accepted there have gone up tenfold. South Africa wants people who work in tourism, while New Zealand welcomes medical staff.

The younger the applicant and the more qualified he or she is, the better the chances of acceptance. Maximum points go to those under 30, minimum to the over-fifties.

The new destination for emigrants is Europe. According to Dudley Baines, reader in economic history at the London School of Economics, free movement within the EU has made the continent an increasingly attractive proposition.

About 58,000 Britons now emigrate to other EU countries, while the numbers for South Africa are about 1,000, 9,000 for Australia and 7,000 for Canada. In Europe, Germany is the most popular destination. About 100,000 UK nationals live there permanently.

Here are the case studies of my five movers:

The ultimate handbook

After a varied professional life which culminated in five years as a computer expert liaising with the *Financial Times* in London, in 1991 Anthony Capstick moved his family back to Whalley, the small town in rural Lancashire in which he was brought up. He set up a company called Instant Search which provides data about companies to clients, instantly. The material is gathered and delivered via computer, so Anthony can work anywhere. His company is based in a converted semi in a side street and now employs four people apart from Anthony and his wife Katie, who gave up her career with US investment house Goldman Sachs when they made the move.

I've gone back to my roots but I've taken with me a lot of experience in terms of working in the City and a high-tech environment, and I've used that to fund my existence in the countryside.

I could have taken the business anywhere but we've our families, our roots here.

I set the business up with a single PC equipped with a fax modem at the foot of the bed in the cottage we moved to when we came up here. We've got to the point now where we are turning over a quarter of a million a year with over 4,000 clients.

The breakthrough came when Companies House went on line, so you could get access to the information they hold without having to physically turn up at their offices in London. That gave me the idea for setting up the business.

I'd always wanted to work for myself, so when we had our first child, Thomas, that was the watershed and we thought it's now or never. I've nothing against cities but we thought we'd prefer to bring him up in the country. We've got two more sons now, William and Robert.

After the bedroom I set up a telecottage, so I have quite a bit of experience of the teleworking concept. It's been five years now and it works fine. But to work for yourself, and from home, you need to have motivation and self-discipline. I'd never have my employees working from home – they come here to work where I can see what they are doing. But home working lends itself to anyone who is paid on a piecemeal basis – architects, designers, journalists.

The quality of life is much better here, especially having a family; the schools, the safety, the lack of pollution, but if you miss the theatre and restaurants it's a loss. I miss the intellectual stimulus of contact with journalists, they do know there is life outside Clitheroe. But e-mail is a great boon. I use it to keep in touch with people. I am in almost daily contact with a pal of mine who is a lecturer at Auckland University.

I'd like to be a multi-millionaire, and then I could have a helicopter and spend some of the time in London and some time in Whalley. It's not a lot to ask is it really!

Financially we were hard up for a while. I was lucky in that my parents were self-employed farmers so I had some inkling of what it would be like. But it was extremely difficult initially. I gave up a secure position with an employer who was notoriously benevolent.

We will stay where we are now and grow the business, continue looking at ways of using the technology to improve what we do and try and get the word out about what we are.

Kevin Attfield is manager in strategic planning for NatWest Bank. He decided to move to Scotland to find a better life for his family – William (12), Rebecca (11), Ruth (8) and Catherine (5). He did so without telling his employer and expected to have to leave the bank and find another job, but the company wanted to keep him and now allow him to work three days a week in London, and telecommute for the other two days.

It was purely by chance that we found ourselves moving to Bute, a smallish island (15 miles long) off the west coast of Scotland in the Firth of Clyde, about 30 miles due west of Glasgow. For some years we had been looking to move but we weren't quite sure where. We were playing with the idea of going abroad, but when we started looking in detail at going to France, say, it just wasn't going to work out – the complications with the culture, the language, schooling and so forth. And in the end we decided that it wasn't a starter so we looked at the West Country. We reached the stage where we had a possible job lined up, we found a buyer for our house and a house to buy but at the last minute everything fell through so we put the whole thing on ice.

Then, I suppose about six months later, we were on holiday in Scotland and it happened to be Bute, which we had visited a number of times before. There was no real ulterior motive, but at the end of the first week we thought, 'Well, this is everything we have been looking for over the past few years.' It came as quite a surprise because it wasn't what we'd expected would appeal to us, with all the possible practical difficulties of living this far away from my work and so forth. But, quite independently, we both realised that this was where we wanted to live.

This wasn't the 'wouldn't it be nice to live here?' type of thought you sometimes get on holiday. This was different. There were so many factors to do with the place, the people and so on. But there was something even deeper than that. But it was absurd, it was 400

Move It

miles away from where I worked, and our families in the south.

I didn't tell my bosses that I was moving until after it had happened, partly because the whole thing was so on-off. I'm slightly ashamed about that. I have worked for NatWest for 14 or 15 years, ever since I graduated. I think it came as quite a shock to them. Not the sort of thing you expect an employee to come in and say on a Monday morning. I didn't see any way of reconciling what I was doing with carrying on working for the bank, and was expecting to have to find a new job in Glasgow, where there are a number of fairly large financial institutions. It was only that the bank had a flexible working practice policy in place that really allowed both sides to get the best of both worlds.

I put in a proposal. My boss came back with a request for more information on the financial side, but generally supported the idea. We started off with two days' teleworking initially and that is how it has stayed. The original plan was to move to three, but two is really the right number for the job.

There are 10 people in the unit I work in. We all have our own jobs to do but work as a team, and my assistant acts as an intermediary.

Teleworking hasn't been too much of an obstacle because I can speak to people on the phone, fax papers back and forth and stay in touch with what's going on. The rest of the week I can see people face-to-face. On Wednesday morning when I get in I have an update meeting with my boss and go through the work and any issues. That's followed by a team meeting. So I don't feel as though I'm not part of the unit, and nor do they.

The arrangement is more sustainable than I originally thought. I'd expected it to grind me down physically *but I've adjusted to the travel and my family has adjusted to the routine.*

To get here I catch a night coach to Glasgow from Victoria Coach Station, then a train for 25 miles to the ferry for the island. I leave London at 11 p.m. and am back on the island at 9 a.m.

Life is much better here. We had a fairly typical modern four-bedroomed detached house with a small garden in Pangbourne, Berkshire and moved to something very much larger. It is a semi-detached Victorian house but the rooms are enormous. Space is very important when you have four children. We also have a very large garden.

In Pangbourne we were part of the village, we had a network of friends there and our families were reasonably close, but it was a very congested sort of area, there was a lot of traffic, there was the question of safety with the kids going out on their own. We didn't like the noise, the pollution and the pace of life. Socially it was very competitive. Quite a materialistic society. We felt we only had half a life there.

There is evidence that Scottish education is better, certainly that is what we believe. We are all fairly outdoorsy. My wife and I like walking on mountains, and the kids all like horse-riding, which we could not afford in Berkshire. We didn't feel as if we had any roots in the southeast. Although we had both been brought up in the area we didn't feel we belonged there.

The children were both apprehensive and enthusiastic. Because we had been visiting the island for a few years before we actually moved it gave us all quite a time to get used to the idea. But when we came to move it was quite a big step, particularly for them. It meant leaving their friends, their school, the way of life they

Move It

knew. My son had some bullying to deal with to begin with at school but he's sorted that out now. The girls made friends pretty quickly and settled in.

Our parents were concerned about the risk and the scale of what we were doing. Obviously it was going to take us further away from them. They are not getting any younger. That was one of the hardest parts to deal with. There is a conflict of loyalties between your responsibilities to your parents and your own children, and we resolved it in this direction, but it's important to say we make more effort to stay in touch. My wife goes down quite regularly and both sets of parents come up a couple of times a year.

There are great benefits to rural communities if a range of professional people can live and work there. If they have the right attitude they can contribute to the economy and the community, get involved in social activities and such like. We are fairly involved, my wife more so because she is here all the time. She is a parent governor at the local school, and as a family we are quite involved in the sailing club. There is always plenty going on, and being a small community you get to know people fairly quickly.

Alan Denbigh quit his job as a software agent, which earned him £30,000 plus a company car and other perks, and took a job for half the money as a project manager developing teleworking for ACRE – Action with Communities in Rural England.

I was prepared to lose half my money in order to work from home. At the time my wife, a producer for the BBC in Bristol, was expecting our first child and I felt the change would be easier on the family. She was already working from home and as we live in a semi-rural area where the transport is crap I decided it would be the best move.

My company were insistent that I stay: when I said that I would be working for a charity, they offered to pay the difference between the two salaries – another £15,000 – to keep me working. But I turned them down.

It's not that I am antisocial, but I just wanted to be more flexible and to get out of the office politics. The company was turning over 50 per cent of its staff every six months, so there was hardly the opportunity to develop a social life with my colleagues.

I feel I'm well out of it, it was so depressing. To work from home doesn't really require a great deal of dedication. Sure, sometimes I say 'sod it' and don't start work until 10.30 a.m., but I still work a conventional day and I don't have all the hassles of spending two hours travelling to work. And I don't spend hours in the pub after work. The work culture is completely different. You can start and finish when you like. Some people feel they work better at 3 a.m., and they can do it.

Jane Palmer left Britain for Germany because her job as an architect was under threat here, but she believed there were healthier prospects on the Continent.

A German friend told me to try finding work in Germany. It was a tough decision because, although job prospects were very poor in Britain with the recession in the building trade, I knew very little about what I would find in Germany. I was 29 and single, so I had no ties here, but I had only a little very rusty German and no contacts.

I stayed with my friend and just hit the telephone directories, calling all the architects practices I could find. My first question to them all had to be 'Do you speak English?' which got the phone slammed down on me a number of times. But eventually I was invited along for an interview with one company.

I got the job, and have been here two years now. Apart from the language and the cultural differences, things were very easy in many ways. My architecture training was easily adaptable and I had no visa to worry about. I had thought about emigrating to an English-speaking country – Australia preferably, but found the bureaucracy too much to cope with. I could probably have got in on a visitor's visa and worked for six months or so, but I very much doubted whether a permanent job could come of it, and what I really wanted was stability.

I don't think I will settle permanently in Germany, but I do enjoy the German way of life. They are very active, they go out a lot and have a good time, and at weekends there is a lot of sporting activity, cycling, skiing and so on. I like all that, and I love being able to hop on a train and be in another country for the weekend. It reminds me of my student days.

Working abroad has really broadened my horizons.

Freelance journalist Alan Smith moved from Ealing, West London, to rural Kent, and loved it. But, while his children settled in well to their new school and his wife found work as a supply teacher, his work dried up. He discovered that, although in terms of technology it was perfectly possible for him to live and work away from London, his clients forgot about him if they did not see his face regularly. So he moved back to town.

We moved to a village halfway between Rye and Tenterden. I had no doubts about the move. My wife Rachel is from the area and we both knew it well. We found a really nice 17th-century cottage for the price of our flat in London, and settled in well. People were friendly, and because I was around the place all day every day I got to know people quite quickly. There was a good school in the next village and my children, Alex (8) and Becky (6), were happy, well-taught and made new friends. Rachel found a reasonable amount of work as a supply teacher and we fixed up an au pair share with another family in the village to help with the children when we were both working.

The problem was an unforeseen one. I had been writing freelance articles on a number of subjects for magazines and newspapers and doing quite a bit of editing and sub-editing. While we were in London I used to do almost all of my work from home, just popping in to offices to drop things off or to hassle for payment, which was always slow as it is for any self-employed person. But, once I had moved, I kept getting asked to pop in for a discussion, or to do some rush piece of editing or page layout. It went down really badly when I said that it would take me two hours to get there. I found the phone rang less and less often.

Also, because I could not be reached by a motorcycle messenger in half an hour as I had been before, people were reluctant to give me projects. Although I had been unaware of it when I lived in London, the fact that I could make physical contact with a company within an hour or so was very important. Objectively, it shouldn't have been. In theory, with my ability to transmit copy electronically and to receive material directly into my home computer, there was no need for me to live close to the offices which employed me.

In the end I found I had to go up to town two or three days a week, and the time wasted in doing so, and *the expense, meant that I could not cope with country life.*

I will regret that the move failed for the rest of my life, but we had to move back. By chance a small house in our old road was up for sale and we were able to buy it. We did not lose out financially, as we were lucky enough to find a buyer in Kent who absolutely fell in love with the cottage and had cash – they paid over the odds to get us out quickly.

I would offer a word of caution to anyone thinking of moving and working from home. They should think much more carefully than I did about what will happen if their faces are not around any longer at work. Like me, they could get forgotten by the people they need to make the move succeed – the ones with the work to offer.

DECISIONS

▼ Is a move essential to your vision of downshifting? If it is, you will need to carry out very careful and thorough research into where you move to. Do you know the place well?

▼ Are you sure the work you intend to do can be carried out effectively from that location?

▼ Can you remain living where you are, or in the same general area, and still fulfil your ambitions?

▼ Have you worked out carefully how much you can afford to spend on your mortgage and other housing expenses, and ensured that you can afford either to move or to live in your present style?

▼ If you feel emigration is the answer, how confident are you that the life you envisage in the country that appeals to you is attainable? Have you looked fully into work prospects? Do you really know what life is like in that country?

The ultimate handbook

CHAPTER TEN

Living without Loads of Money

The key question to address now is this: Can you support yourself in the new, downshifted lifestyle which you are planning?

If you have followed the programme mapped out in the previous chapters you will have constructed for yourself an outline of the sort of life you wish to lead. You will have decided where your paid work will come from. You will have decided whether you are to construct a portfolio of activities for yourself or whether you are going to start a business and achieve your goals through that. You will have decided whether you are to spend some of your time studying, whether you intend to do some unpaid charitable work and whether you intend to move to a new house, area or country.

What every downshifter needs to do now is to take the pieces of the jigsaw which until now have been dealt with in isolation and bring them together to see if they make a coherent whole. First, a whole that works, that you feel will satisfy and fulfil you, and secondly, whether the whole picture makes financial sense. This is the bottom line: Will your downshifted lifestyle leave you in the red, or in the black?

Here are three examples of ways in which downshifters have worked out that equation.

Simon Strong has given up a full-time, demanding job as a computer programmer and replaced it with a portfolio of 20 hours a week paid work as a technical author, five hours studying for a horticultural qualification, five hours helping in his children's school and approximately 15 hours looking after his children; his wife, Melanie, is working towards starting up an antiques business. The family has trimmed their spending to live on just over half the income they enjoyed previously.

Graeme Glass has just given up employment as an equities salesman in the City and sold everything to start his own business as an importer of Indian antiques.

Sandy Fielding and her husband Derek both switched to work part-time for the Civil Service. They had to move to a cheaper home, sell their car, and make other financial sacrifices, but are delighted with the extra time they now have to be together with their young family.

What is absolutely vital is that you have your finances in order before you downshift.

In Chapter 2 we dealt with assessing the minimum on which you could happily live. In the chapters since, you've been given the chance to try to work out what income you can expect. Now comes the crunch – seeing whether what you can realistically earn matches what you need.

Take the calculation you made in Chapter 2 of the minimum expenditure you feel you can live on (*see page 33*). Compare it to the new income level that you expect once you have downshifted. Do the figures balance?

It is quite possible that they won't, on a first calculation. Which means you will have to go back and see if anything can be cut, and try to balance the equation again. If you cannot come up with a way of cutting your spending to

The ultimate handbook

fit your new, downshifted income, then the sorry conclusion must be that downshifting is not an option for you at present. There is no point settling for what is, to you, an unacceptably low standard of living, because you simply won't be happy and the benefits of downshifting will be outweighed by the drawbacks.

But there is much that can be done to trim expenditure, often in ways that you will hardly notice or which, at the very least, will not be too painful to bear. Most of us waste a good deal of money, or spend it in ways designed to compensate for the pressures our work puts us under. Remove the pressures and the need for the spending evaporates.

It will be a hugely worthwhile exercise if, as you plan your move to downshifting, you experiment with living on half your income, and see how it feels.

I persuaded two families to do just that for a week, and record how much money they saved and how much of a hardship they found the experience.

Here, broken down into the four main areas of household expenditure, is what they did to save money, and how much they cut their bills by:

FOOD

They switched to supermarket own brands and budget lines. The quality may be slightly lower, but the food is still nutritional. Breakfasts consisted of cereal or porridge, puddings were fruit. They cut out expensive cuts of meat, substituting cheaper ones and vegetarian dishes, as vegetables are far cheaper than meat. They took packed lunches to work instead of buying sandwiches or restaurant meals. They avoided going to the pub or wine bar at lunch time or after work.

By doing all this, these two families cut their weekly food bills from, respectively, £120 a week to £45 and £115 to £30.

Cooking for yourself is almost always cheaper than eating out. The drawback is it takes time to shop for and prepare a meal, but most downshifters will have more time to do so, so trying it now is a good idea. If cooking becomes a pleasure, that's a bonus; if not, you should perhaps bear this in mind and put it into the equation as to whether you should downshift or not.

TRANSPORT

On short journeys, my families left the car at home and walked or cycled. Both said that cutting out the 10 short school trips a week through rush hour traffic cut petrol consumption noticeably, though the children hated being made to walk!

They used public transport to get to work. One husband, who commutes by rail, walked to the station, saving on car parking charges as well as petrol.

My two guinea pig families cut spending from £29.50 to £3 and £25 to £10 respectively.

HOUSEHOLD BILLS

Savings here were made by switching off lights and turning the central heating down by a degree or two and reducing the hours it was on. The families used a range of other measures, such as using the economy setting on the washing machine and a clothes rack instead of an electric dryer, and washing up by hand instead of using the dish washer. Savings were from £66 to £12 and from £18 to £10.

ENTERTAINMENT AND GENERAL SPENDING

The families ate out less, and at less expensive places when they did. They borrowed books and CDs from the library

The ultimate handbook

and rented videos rather than going to the cinema. They cut spending from £197 to £41 and from £85 to £39 a week.

The key to being frugal is planning ahead and being organised. If you plan menus you can more easily avoid waste by using leftovers in subsequent dishes, for example. But too much self-denial can be counter-productive. If you take all the fun out of life you are defeating one of the prime objects in downshifting. The families who helped me with this experiment were amazed at how much money they could save each week and, while they felt they had probably gone further than was sustainable week-in week-out, they both accepted that substantial cuts were perfectly easy to make. Living on half the expenditure they normally made would be quite easy, they both felt.

This was just a very short-term experiment. While all the advice above holds for the long term, there is much that can supplement it.

For example, in the area of household bills, here are 10 tips which will help you to save more than £100 on energy in a year.

1 Only use the heat, lights and appliances you need
   Savings: £15–£40 annually

2 Lag your hot water tank
   Cost: £5–£10   Savings: £15–£40 annually

3 Lag your pipes
   Cost: £5–£10   Savings: £5–£10 annually

4 Use low-energy light bulbs
   Cost: £8–£17   Savings: £12 annually

5 Add thermostatic radiator valves
   Cost: £45–£75   Savings: £10–£20 annually
   Adding timer programmes costs £35–£40, saves
   £20–£25. Turning the thermostat down by 1° saves
   on average £30 with electricity, £35 with gas, annually

6 Fit draught proofing to windows and doors
   Cost: £45–£50   Savings: £10–£20

7 Insulate your loft
   Cost: £110 for   Savings: £60–£70 annually
   DIY–£300 for contractor

8 Install plastic secondary double glazing
   Cost: £120–£600   Savings: £15–£25 annually

9 Cavity wall insulation
   Cost: £300–£500   Savings: £60–£70 annually

10 Replace old, wasteful central heating boiler with a
   new one
   Cost: £400–£600   Savings: £100 to £130 annually

There are all sorts of other ways of saving money, and many of them will flow directly and painlessly from your decision to downshift. The clothes, car and other paraphernalia that went with your previous lifestyle may no longer be necessary. You will have much more time to do things for yourself rather than paying others to do them for you. There will be no more handymen, cleaners or nannies to pay, but there will be many new chores for you to do.

One essential before you downshift is that you clear your debts. It is hard enough living on a reduced salary, without paying for luxuries bought in your 'previous life'. It can help enormously if you have some savings behind you. If you know, for instance, that there is enough in the bank to see you through your first year then that can be a great comfort.

One financial element that can often spur a person to consider downshifting seriously is the offer of a voluntary redundancy package. Particularly if you intend to start a business, or need a lump sum to reduce your mortgage substantially, voluntary redundancy can make downshifting a viable option. But you must look carefully into what terms are being offered. Many middle managers leave with several tens of thousands of pounds, but that reflects their companies' desire to induce them to go, rather than any legal requirement. The amount of cash that must legally be paid to those made redundant – the bare statutory minimum – is not that great. It is calculated on the following basis:

One-and-a-half weeks' pay for each complete year of employment in which the employee is between the age of 41 and 65. But this is based on a maximum of £210 a week (at the time of writing).

One week's pay for each complete year of employment in which the employee is between the ages of 22 and 41.

Half a week's pay for each complete year of employment in which the employee is between the ages of 18 and 22.

The maximum number of years' service that counts towards statutory redundancy payments is 20, and you are only entitled to a payment if you have been employed for at least two years.

Other points to bear in mind are that if the employee is to get a company pension, part of it can be offset against the redundancy payout.

Many employers also offer outplacement, a process of support and counselling, as part of the redundancy package. Many people are offered a choice between outplacement and more cash, and most of them opt for the money. If you are

Living without Loads of Money

fairly confident about your future plans, this is probably the right choice. But if you want another job, outplacement is of proven benefit. Research by DBM, the world's largest outplacement company, shows that 70 per cent of those who undertake it find jobs at the same or a higher salary, while other research shows that those who don't take outplacement are three times more likely to be out of work after 12 months.

If you think your job is under threat, start planning your financial future now.

If you have done that and a redundancy package is offered, or forced upon you, you should be as well-equipped as possible to benefit from it.

If you are financially secure and plan to reduce your working hours or start a business, you should find the cash a great help. But don't rush into anything. Put the lump sum into the bank or building society while you plan your next move. It is tempting to pay off the mortgage, and a good idea once you know that you will not need the cash for some other venture, but don't do it until you've explored your future plans as thoroughly as you can.

Finally, it is well worth seeing a financial adviser. An independent adviser who can run an experienced eye over your whole financial situation and tell you how healthy or otherwise it is can save you from all sorts of expensive mistakes. His or her services will not be cheap – around £80 per hour probably – but they are worth it.

Now let's look at this chapter's case studies in full:

Simon Strong has switched to a new job which he does for 20 hours a week. His wife Melanie sells antiques.
I had the classic high-pressure, high-reward job with a major computer company. I took voluntary redundancy from that job and got a £40,000 lump sum. That

The ultimate handbook

came straight off the mortgage, cutting our debt from £100,000 to £60,000 and the repayments by a similar proportion. That was what made downshifting possible. I was given outplacement training which showed me that I had an ability as a teacher and author, and I now work part-time for a company which produces instruction manuals for software companies. The work is new to me and I love it. The pay is only £15,000, which is £20,000 less than I was earning before. I had a company car in my job and we have not replaced it. We both share Melanie's car now, an eight-year-old Golf, and there have been a few other sacrifices. We spend less on clothes now, and on incidentals such as wine bar lunches and drinks in the pub after work – which add up massively.

Melanie has always been interested in antiques and has now started trying to build up a business. Her interest is Victorian jewellery and she has a stall in a local craft market and goes to craft antique fairs around the country. She seems to have a real flair for the business and is beginning to show a profit. It is possible that, if things go well, she will want to open a shop, and that could boost our income.

I love the free time I have. I have split it in various ways. I am studying horticulture one afternoon and one evening a week at my local further education college for an HND and also a diploma in garden design. This is just a hobby at this stage, but could perhaps develop into a money-making venture in a few years.

Then, for an average of five hours a week, I help out at my son Sam's school. Melanie is doing a two-days a week course in French at college as well, and I look after Sam when she is studying.

I suppose we are now living on half the money we had before, once you take reduced mortgage payments and so on into account. Life is certainly more spartan, but much more enjoyable. The only thing I miss is being able to buy good claret, which I have a passion for. Now I have to rely on supermarket plonk.

Graeme Glass switched from the City to importing Indian artefacts. He is single, without commitments, and lives in Goudhurst, Kent.

I was 35 and earning a salary well into six figures as a Japanese equities salesman, but I could not see where I was headed.

I went to India on holiday and fell in love with furniture from the days of colonialism. I was sure there would be a market for it, it is wonderful stuff, antique but with a slightly rough-hewn ethnic appeal. I came back, resigned and sold everything I had. There was a flat in Pimlico, a cottage in Wiltshire, the contents of both and quite a good collection of lithographs. All told I realised about £450,000 and I poured all of it into buying stock, shipping it, warehousing it and finding retail outlets.

At first it was a disaster. Battling with bureaucracy and corruption was a nightmare. Some of the outlets were worse than useless. The furniture didn't fit in with the English antiques they were selling alongside it, and it took time to find the right places to sell to. At one point I was literally broke, but I was determined not to go back into the City. Thank God I had never borrowed money, I am sure no bank manager would have stuck with me.

I work far harder now than I ever did as an employee, and the stress is enormous. I can't think of having a

The ultimate handbook

serious relationship, and a family is therefore right off the map, which is beginning to worry me as I am 37. But I have no real regrets. I feel like I am now in the real world.

Sandy Fielding and her husband Derek work part-time for the Civil Service so they can share the upbringing of their twins, Anne and Jessica.

I went part-time when the twins were born three years ago. That suited me fine, I like my work very much but I also want to be with my family. Derek was different, though. He was a fast-streamer in the Civil Service. They are the stars, expected to solve any problem. Be the brightest in the office and the most creative and quick-thinking. The reward is fast promotion. Derek's hours were not long, only about 45 a week, but that's nine more than he was paid for. Nevertheless, at the end of every day he was totally drained because he was under such pressure at the office. Once he was sick, with what he called flu but which I think was exhaustion, and took 10 days off. He got calls almost daily, ostensibly to check that he was OK, but really to pressure him into returning to work. Then Anne had an accident. She slipped on an icy path at school and broke her arm. I took her to hospital and phoned Derek, but it was two hours before his boss would allow him out of a meeting to come to his daughter.

That night we discussed what to do. We both realised it was the final straw. Derek asked to be demoted to the lowest management grade and to cut his hours from 36 to 30 a week. His salary was cut from £24,500 to £19,000, the same as mine. We thought hard about whether we would cope financially, because up till then we had always lived at the limit of our expenditure. We

Living without Loads of Money

bought our house in Wandsworth in 1988, at the height of the housing boom, and were suffering from negative equity. We sold our car and bought a much cheaper and older one, and cut down on how much we use it. We used to like to eat out regularly and we've had to stop that. We don't buy nearly as many clothes as we used to, and money is always tight. But it doesn't matter. Now we can take the girls to school and pick them up, and there is usually one of us around to be with them. Our priorities have changed. Family and hobbies are top of the agenda now. Derek has much greater self-esteem. All his ambition is now directed into things like being a good father, and he is a better person for it.

DECISIONS

This really is decision time. You have your new life mapped out. Now you must decide whether it works. Will you be happy with it? Does it make financial sense?

Sort out your balance sheet. Compare what you are likely to earn in the future with your calculations of the minimum you can live on. If the figures don't tally at first, go back over them and see if you can make any further cuts. If you can balance your budget, downshifting is a viable option. If you cannot, you need to think again.

CHAPTER ELEVEN

Time Is on Your Side

I BEGAN this book by talking about the moment at which people choose to downshift, that point at which they decide enough is enough and they must change their lives.

But few do anything on the spur of the moment. After the decision is taken to seek out a new, different way of living and working, it may be a year or more before they are ready to act on it. In the mean time they will prepare carefully, for the key to successful downshifting is preparedness.

You must know when to make your move. You must give yourself the time to adjust your financial and other commitments. Maybe you'll need a couple of years to save hard and reduce your mortgage. If you and your partner both work, you may be able to bank one salary and live on the other to build up your savings and soften the transition to living on far less than you once did.

You must decide upon your transition strategy. Set yourself a timetable so that you can prepare yourself gradually for the move – psychologically as well as in terms of adequate finances and perhaps a new job. Set a 'departure date', a time limit by which you will have things in place, and keep to it. Then, when you finally downshift, you will be confident and prepared.

Here are three examples of downshifting timetables:

Tom and Claire Keepsie worked hard to halve their mortgage and cut the salary they needed by half. It was two years before downshifting became a realistic possibility.

Karen Beith had always longed to teach, but had left school without A levels. She did A levels at evening school, and saved hard to support herself through her full-time teacher training course.

Jim Waite put by enough to launch his own personnel management consultancy before he gave up his old job.

Your timetable will start to become apparent once you pull together all the decisions you have made while working your way through this book.

For instance, you will have worked out in Chapter 2 the bare minimum you can live on. You will have decided how long it will take you to reduce your debt to an appropriate level for your new income. This may take time. It may, indeed, be the one governing factor in when you are ready to downshift.

In Chapter 5 you will have decided what sort of paid employment you wish to find. You may have to wait until you can organise a new, less demanding job. It may be that, for you, the key is the right employment opening – a vacancy in the company you wish to work for. Or perhaps you are waiting for conditions to be right within your present company to request to go part-time, or apply for voluntary redundancy.

If you are to start a business, any number of factors may dictate the pace at which you are able to move towards your goal.

If you need to study for new qualifications, the length of the course you have to take may be the deciding factor in when you can make the break.

If you are to move house then you may be in the hands of the housing market.

However many factors there are governing your downshift, it is important to list them in order of importance. Then, you can work through the problems one by one. If the most important factor is cutting your debt, you need to set a target date for when that will be achieved, and a strategy for achieving it. You can then gear other things – getting a new qualification, asking to go part-time at work – to that.

Tom and Claire Keepsie's problem was a £130,000 mortgage. They knew that if they were to downshift they had to work twice as hard as they had been up until then. Claire got a full-time job and they banked her salary. With the lump sum they saved over the next two years, and by cashing in a share option Tom had received as part of his employment package, they took £70,000 off the mortgage, cutting their repayments by more than half.

We decided we needed to bring in £40,000 a year between us, which was exactly half of my then salary. The big cost was the mortgage, at almost £1,000 a month. We decided that we had to halve those repayments, and to do that we had to save between £60,000 and £70,000. We did it by Claire getting a full-time job, which netted her £25,000 a year, all of which we banked. It took two years to get the money together. During that time we got used to living on far less. We had always been free spenders – entertaining, eating very well and going on three or four holidays a year. We stopped all that and took a very close look at every penny we spent. By the time we were ready to push the button and downshift, we were spending £2,000 a month rather than the £3,500 we'd been getting through before.

In the two years Claire found she loved her job in television production and wanted to keep working full-time. That was fine by me, as I had carried on working while she took breaks to have our two children, Penelope and Joseph, and, while my ambitions were largely fulfilled, hers were not. I became a freelance contributor to my old newspaper, working two or three days a week, and took over primary child care.

Karen Beith had to save up for three years before she had enough to support herself through a four-year teacher training course.

I left school at 16 and became a secretary. Then I moved into telesales and finally I was managing a whole team of telesales people. The job was demanding, with constant targets to hit. I was well paid, but unfulfilled. I longed to teach, but the problem would obviously be affording to study for four years to get a BEd.

I also had to get my A levels, so I combined studying at night school with saving hard. It took me three years to get my A levels, and in that time I had saved £15,000. My colleagues at work thought I had gone mad. One minute I was the life and soul of the party, out with them in the wine bar every night, off on weekends away, but suddenly I stopped all that and went into my shell. At first they thought I must be pining over some man, and I didn't tell them what I was doing in case they thought that with my new goals I would not be giving enough to the job. I made sure that I worked even harder than usual so no one could say I had lost my motivation.

The ultimate handbook

*When I finally resigned after three years' prepara-
tion my bosses would not believe that I was going to
college. They thought I had been head-hunted for some
brilliant new job – they kept trying to find out if I had
'joined the opposition' as they called it, by which they
meant working for a rival magazine group.*

*I had few commitments to consider. I was single
and I had never bought property, so I had nothing to
sell, and moved into shared student digs when I went to
university. It was strange doing that, being with 18 year
olds when I was 26, but I got used to it. I worked in a
bar and a restaurant to support myself through university.*

*Without the period of preparation I don't think I
could have stood being a poor student. I am glad I took
time to get used to the idea of not spending every penny
I earned. I think preparing like that is the key to why
I managed to stick it successfully. I didn't plan it like
that, of course, it was a necessity, but it was certainly
for the best.*

Jim Waite was a senior personnel manager for a building society. He spent much of his time helping staff to
cope with redundancy, and finally realised that his own
job was becoming more and more precarious. He was-
n't sure when the push would come, but decided to start
making his own preparations for what work he would
do when he was let go. He was glad that he did.

*I was 45 and had been in personnel management
for six years. To be honest, although I was responsible
for seeing hundreds and hundreds of staff made redundant, advising them on what to do and hopefully making the experience as painless as is possible, it was not
me who saw my own redundancy coming. It was my
wife, Eileen, who said to me one day – 'If it goes on like*

this there will be no one else to sack, and you will have nothing to do all day.' When I thought about it I realised she was right, so I began to plan.

I could not say with any certainty at all when they would let me go, but I reckoned I had a couple of years. As it turned out, I went after 14 months. I would have liked more time to prepare, but at least when I did get the push I knew exactly what new line of work I would undertake.

I decided that I would become a one-man personnel management consultancy. Many firms, including a lot of those I knew about in the world of banking and finance, were putting out personnel management to outside organisations. I began to build up a data-base of all those who were doing so, and of others who, I thought, ought to consider it. I could not approach anyone, but I was accumulating invaluable leads for when I was out on my own.

I got a year's salary from the bank – £26,000 – which wiped out the mortgage. We had been in the same house since we were married, 20 years ago, so there wasn't that much left to repay. I thought about working from home but, as I had some cash and wanted to keep home and work separate, I rented a small office half a mile away from home.

My preparation worked brilliantly. On the first day I started cold-calling all those companies I had identified as possibly needing my services. Right in the first week I got some interest, and after three weeks I got my first contract. I have been at it for almost a year now, and am keeping my head above water. So far I have not had to touch the rest of my pay-off other than the £5,000 I used to set up my office. I would find it a disappointment to have to dip into that – an admission of

The ultimate handbook

partial failure. I am sure that in a year's time I will be well and truly established.

DECISIONS

When will you downshift? Take all the considerations discussed above into account and set a date for when you will take the plunge. Pencil in key dates along the road, so that you can see whether you are meeting the timetable you have set yourself.

CHAPTER TWELVE

The Future

THE first day in your new, downshifted life can be a strange
one. Certainly, no one I have spoken to has ever forgotten it,
or the odd mix of fear and exhilaration that they felt as it
dawned on them that, finally, they had made the break and
invented a new life for themselves.

Many speak of experiencing a sobering feeling of being
on their own. Many of the support mechanisms of their previous lives have been withdrawn. Many downshifters work
from home, and find that an eerie silence descends on the
house during the day, which is in stark contrast to the bustle
of office life. There is no one to gossip with at the coffee
machine, no one to ask for advice about a problem, no one
to go for a drink with and slag off the boss to. Your setbacks
and your triumphs are borne in isolation. You fall back on
to your own resources far more than you used to.

Any problems that you encounter are likely to arise
within the first few months, as the three downshifters we
meet in this chapter can testify:

Steven Mays left his local council's direct works organisation, where he was a gardener, and set up his own
one-man garden design and maintenance business. For

him, the hardest part was the loss of his colleagues. It was six months before he came to terms with the loneliness.

Alice Fenby took early retirement from her job as a music teacher in a junior school and set up in her own home as a piano teacher. She found that in the first year her business built painfully slowly, and that nothing she did to advertise her services had any effect. Finally, she had to accept that word of mouth was the only advertising that worked for her. It took 12 months before she had enough pupils to make an acceptable living.

Tim Lees gave up his job as a travelling salesman for a drug company in order to do a degree in psychology. But when his wife lost her job there was not enough money to fund his studies. He had to drop out for a year and work on a building site before he could resume his studies.

One of the problems downshifters face in Britain is that they are a pioneering breed. There are not, as yet, that many of them – though their ranks are swelling by the day. In the US it is different. Over the past decade the downshifting movement – which, over there, goes by a number of different names, including 'the voluntary simplicity movement' – has become a major force.

The statistics bear this out, although findings of the extent of downshifting can vary widely, depending on the questions asked and the respondents chosen. A survey conducted for the magazine *US News and World Report*, for example, showed that 48 per cent of Americans had taken steps in the previous five years to simplify their lives, including cutting back their hours at work and declining promotion. A slightly higher figure, 51 per cent, said time was more important to them than money. In a survey of its own employees, the Du Pont corporation found that 21 per cent of its staff had refused overtime or a job with more pressure over the past 10 years. A Merck Family Fund survey found that 66 per cent of Americans would be happier if they were able to spend more time with family and friends, and 28 per cent of respondents were doing something about it. They, the survey reported, had voluntarily made changes in their lives that resulted in lower earnings in order to have a more balanced life. But the survey revealed figures which show that, even in the US, downshifting is by no means the way everybody is going. For 33 per cent of respondents had 'upshifted' to a higher standard of living.

Dr Juliet Schor, a Harvard economist and author of *The Overworked American*, says that the voluntary simplicity movement 'is exploding, growing very rapidly, mushrooming'. The *Trends Journal* called it one of the top trends of the nineties and predicted that it would attract 15 per cent of baby boomers by the year 2000.

Such figures at least lend credence to the view that a profound value shift may be at work. And, where the US leads, much of the rest of the world follows. Of course, the US has got a good deal further down the road of consumer excess than even western Europe, but that is no reason why we may not learn from their mistakes.

We can also look to the pro-downshifting infrastructure that has developed in some American cities, and learn from it. Seattle is a pioneering centre for those who wish to downshift. The city has seen a good deal of the phenomenon because of its own particular employment pattern. In the 1990s many computer and other high-tech firms came to the city, drawing with them very bright, ambitious high achievers. But in the nineties those industries have been shedding workers in large numbers.

Suddenly, there were many highly qualified men and women in Seattle who were either sacked or offered voluntary redundancy. Increasingly, others are seeing the writing on the wall and downshifting of their own volition. Many of them had fallen in love with Seattle's beautiful scenery and slower pace of life and decided to stay. So a complex network has sprung up among those who have downshifted. There are newsletters dedicated to the simple life, and support groups attended by those who wish to make the break. As you might expect in the US, they take it all deadly seriously – ascribing whole-heartedly to the view that breaking away from reliance on a job is as emotionally wrenching and physically demanding as withdrawal from an addiction to drugs or alcohol.

At a support group meeting you might find, for example, a college administrator, the founder of a computer company, and a civil servant among those sitting in a circle. As each in turn introduces themselves they say: 'My interest is in getting out of the rat race and getting back to simplicity' and the statement is greeted with whoops of encouragement.

Somehow I can't see we Brits embracing the encounter-session approach to downshifting, but it is a very good idea to make contact with any fellow downshifters you can find in your area, to share problems, exchange moans and generally offer some replacement for the workmates you have left behind.

In Seattle, neighbourhood coffee shops and bookshops have sprung up which cater for those who have downshifted, who want to come in with their lap-top computers and sit all morning over a coffee or use the bookshop as a research centre and meeting place. Seattle's public library has even prepared a resource list for downshifters which includes literary accounts, economics texts and lifestyle handbooks.

There are neighbourhood 'simplicity circles' springing up – groups devoted to exploiting lower-stress, lower-cost lifestyles and giving practical advice and assistance.

There are also things called community exchanges. These are barter organisations in which the members exchange work or goods for the things that they need. If you are a painter and decorator and you need your car fixed, you may offer to paint the mechanic's kitchen in exchange for a full service on your car. To make the exchange of goods easier, groups often invent their own currency, a sort of toy money which can be used to 'pay' for services and which is accepted by all the members of the group.

The inventor of community exchanges was Olaf Egeberg who, in 1992, founded the Philadelphia-Eastern Neighbourhood (PEN) Exchange in Tacoma Park, Maryland. It began with just 11 residents trading goods and services. Now there are 317 people bartering everything from computer skills to home tutoring and construction work. In lieu of cash payment they trade in their own local currency. In Ithaca, New York, the residents have printed their own 'Ithaca money'. Instead of monetary denominations, the notes are marked in Ithaca Hours. In Kansas City, they have invented the Barter Buck. The concept is being explored in 400 other communities in 48 states.

One great thing about exchange systems is that they do not involve the payment of tax, a great saving when cash is tight.

Another great aid for downshifting Americans are newsletters such as the *Tightwad Gazette*, a monthly publication based in Maine with a circulation of 50,000. It and other newsletters like it, serve as a practical guide to cutting down expenses and living a simpler life.

The editor of the *Gazette*, Amy Dacyczyn, started it after she and her husband, a retired military officer, saved $49,000 in seven years out of a combined income of $30,000. Amy thought that what she had done was something most people didn't believe was possible. She went to lengths that many people will find unacceptable, such as allowing her six children to pick only one new Christmas present a year and buying most of her clothes, toys and household goods from secondhand stores and jumble sales. Ironically, the profit from the *Gazette*, plus book spin-offs, is bringing in a six-figure income, but she has resisted the temptation to develop the business. In fact she intends to close the *Gazette* down because, she says, it has said everything it needs to say about downshifting.

So, at 40, she is planning her retirement – or, rather, a second bout of downshifting. She will restore furniture, make quilts, read novels, look into her family history and become a volunteer.

It is up to individual downshifters to create and foster the same kinds of resources and support here in Britain. Certainly, judging by the experiences of the downshifters I have spoken to, such support mechanisms can be a great comfort.

If you do hit hard times, you will need to draw on your resilience and determination, and all the other strengths identified in Chapter 2.

The worst thing can be the experience of sitting before a silent phone. You have done everything you can to advertise your new venture, you have prepared your contacts and clients, and you expect them to share some of your excitement that you have finally made the break. Somehow, they seem not to have noticed.

The only thing to do is to get out and sell yourself and your services – relentlessly if necessary. Always expect to have to make the first move, to make things happen. If you have moved to a new area, waste no time in getting involved with the local community. Walk around with a smile plastered on your face. It is better to be seen as the new lunatic in town than the new grump. Introduce yourself to neighbours and everyone you come into contact with. If your

The ultimate handbook

children are finding it hard to adapt and make new friends, get to know the parents and then invite them and their children round.

You probably won't be greeted with open arms at first, but be patient. Accept that there can be a greater degree of reserve in small communities than there is in cities. You will eventually be seen for the pleasant, helpful soul that you are!

Setbacks and disappointments are part of the deal when you downshift. Try not to let them knock your confidence. Remember your goals and work doggedly towards them. It is important to look to the long term as a way of keeping current, short-term difficulties in perspective. You can afford to be flexible in the short term, as long as your ultimate ambitions are not affected. For example, you might have to take any work that is going for a few weeks if the work you really want to do is simply not as plentiful as it should be. It is worth it to pay the bills. If you can't see beyond your present difficulties, you risk failing in your long-term aims.

And remember, part of your success in your fast-track life was due to the fact that you took your work so seriously, because you cared about it, worried over it and – when you hit an insurmountable problem or an impossible deadline – used your nervous energy, your fear even, to win through. It is often after a sleepless night following a fruitless day in which none of your calls has been returned and none of your leads has borne fruit that you make the call which connects you with someone who does need your services, who can offer you the work you need.

Fear is a great tool, so use it as the spur to urge yourself on to success. Use pride as well to steel yourself not to give in.

Here are the tales of the setbacks and problems of three downshifters, and how they were surmounted:

Steven Mays' one-man garden maintenance and design business took off almost instantly, but he found he hated working alone so much that he considered packing it in. But success was to provide a solution:

I had expected it would take time to get the business off the ground, but in fact it proved very easy. I had been doing odd gardening jobs and a bit of design in my free time, and so I had a few customers whom I knew would stick by me. But I then had a brilliant breakthrough. One of the local garden centres changed hands and I approached the new owners, who were selling turf, top soil, garden paving and so on, to ask if they were interested in adding a design service. I argued it would boost their sales, and they agreed to give it a go. It worked better than I could ever have hoped, and I was working all the hours I wanted to within a month of going self-employed.

What I found very hard was working alone. At the council there was a big team of us. I was a supervisor in charge of 10 men, and we were a great team. We were growing vast amounts of bedding plants and filling all the parks, borders and traffic islands with blooms. It was lovely work and we had a great time doing it. There was always someone to have a laugh with, to go to the pub with at lunch time or after work.

Coming from that, working on my own felt incredibly lonely. I took to popping into the pub my old colleagues used, but it wasn't the same once I had left. They had a new boss and things were different. I could not get used to that feeling of being on my own. I thought I would start talking to myself and go crazy.

But now I have a solution. My success has been such that I have hired one of my old workmates to help me out. With the two of us there is always someone to

*chat to, which is a great relief. I've realised that no way
am I a loner. I can't work like that, it's just not worth it.
I would have seriously considered packing it in if things
had not worked out like this.*

Alice Fenby's new work as a piano instructor grew
painfully slowly, and she had to do other work to make
ends meet before it finally picked up.

*Of course I knew a good deal of children who were
interested in music when I took early retirement, and
I had discreetly sounded out the parents of those I
thought would be interested in piano lessons with me.
I hoped they would form the bedrock of my venture,
and they did. But there were not enough of them.*

*I had to supplement my income by offering private
tuition in other subjects, which I really did not enjoy.
I was a crammer for children who looked like they might
not pass the entry examinations for local private
schools, or who might fail their GCSEs. Most of them
were just not up to their parents' expectations for them,
which was all rather sad and difficult to deal with.
I began to feel surrounded by failure – with my own
plonked in the middle.*

*Music was the thing I loved and yet I was only able
to teach it for a proportion of the week because there
was simply not the demand for my services. I tried
everything I could to get new pupils, advertising in the
local community newspaper, putting cards in newsagents
and so on. In the end it was word of mouth that proved
to be the best advertisement. Slowly pupils would bring
in their friends, sometimes their parents, for lessons. It
took a year or perhaps slightly more, but now I do not
have to teach anything other than music, which is what
I always wanted.*

I'm so glad, looking back, that I did not give up.

Tim Lees' ambition to complete a psychology degree took a blow when his wife, who was the sole breadwinner while he studied, lost her job.

I had been an area rep for a major drug company in the northwest of England for five years, and by the time I was 31 I was going mad with boredom. I was on the road all the time, driving hundreds of miles and going to dozens and dozens of surgeries. I hated it, and we saw a way out when my wife, Jenny, was able to go back to work when our children were all at school. We have John (10), Sam (9) and Elaine (7).

Jenny got a job as manager of a health food shop in Preston, not far from the house. With her money and some savings, I could finally achieve my ambition and study for a psychology degree. I got a place at Lancaster University, which was close enough for me to commute. Everything went wonderfully for the first nine months or so, but then Jenny got made redundant. There was nothing for it but to talk to the university authorities and explain that I could not afford to go on with the course. They were very understanding and suggested I took a year's break. That way, I was not giving up on my ambition, just deferring things to try and put the finances back in order and continue towards my ultimate goal.

I took a job on a building site for the whole of the summer just so we had some money coming in to put food on the table. It was not until the November that Jenny managed to find herself another job and I could go back to university.

It was very tempting to give up when everything went pear-shaped. I knew I could go back to the sort of work I was doing before, but I hated the idea of that.

I am very glad that Jenny and I kept our eye on the ball. She was better than me, she never wavered at all. She said right along that we would sort it out – and we did.

Finally, let me leave you with something that countless successful downshifters have told me: there is a third great moment in the life of every successful downshifter. We have covered the first, when you decide you must break out, and the second, when you actually put your plans into action. The third is best of the lot. It is when you wake up one morning and realise that you have made it, that your new life works and that your ambitions have been achieved.

Throughout it all, through all the problems, hardships, setbacks and failures, keep your eye on that third magic moment – and work towards it with every scrap of energy, determination and will-power that you possess.

RESOURCES

Here is a range of the most useful sources of information for the downshifter. It is not an exhaustive list, but it should provide every downshifter with a few starting points from which they can begin to build up information tailored to their own personal requirements.

WORK

HOME RUN
Magazine for home workers.

Contact: Andrew James and Sophie Chalmers, Cribau Mill, Llanvair Discoed, Chepstow, Gwent NP6 6RD; tel: 01291 641 222

NEW WAYS TO WORK
For: Advice for workers and employers on flexible working hours, job-sharing, term-time working, career breaks, voluntarily reduced working time, sabbaticals, working from home.

The organisation publishes a series of booklets and factsheets on various aspects of job-sharing and other flexible working arrangements, runs a variety of seminars, training sessions and presentations on job-sharing and flexible working, and publishes a quarterly newsletter with up-to-date information on flexible working arrangements.

Contact: New Ways to Work, 309 Upper Street, London N1 2TY; tel: 0171 226 4026

Teleworking

BRITISH TELECOM

For: A range of booklets about teleworking.
Contact: 0800 800 854

MERCURY COMMUNICATIONS

For: Information for teleworkers and on working from home.
Contact: 0500 500 194

NATIONAL ASSOCIATION OF TELEWORKERS

For: Advice and guidance on working from home.
Contact: 01404 42327

THE TELECOTTAGE ASSOCIATION

For: Support for those who work from home via computer and who use the services of local telecottages. It publishes a magazine, *The Teleworker*, which has full details of around 150 telecottages and how to contact them; also offers discounts on teleworking products, news of new work opportunities, and an advice service.

Contact: The Telecottage Association, WREN Telecottage, Stoneleigh Park, Warwickshire CV8 2RR

Contact The Teleworker *at:* The Other Cottage, Shortwood, Nailsworth, Gloucestershire GL6 OSH; tel: 01453 834 874; fax: 01453 836 174

Starting a Business

BUSINESS LINKS
For: A full range of customised business support services.
   Contact: 0800 400 200

CHAMBERS OF COMMERCE
For: A range of business services for members including education and training, trade promotion, representation. For details of your local branch:
   Contact: 0171 222 1555

CHARTERED INSTITUTE OF MARKETING
For: Advice on all aspects of marketing and selling.
   Contact: 01628 852 145

COMPANIES HOUSE
For: Advice on statutory obligations of company directors, including filing annual returns and accounts. Responsible for holding records on all companies and making them available to the public.
   Contact: 01222 380 801

CUSTOMS AND EXCISE
For: Information on importing, exporting, customs duty, excise duty and VAT.
   Contact: 0171 202 4227 for Customs and Excise inquiries
   0171 202 4087 for VAT inquiries

DEPT OF TRADE AND INDUSTRY AND FOREIGN AND COMMONWEALTH OFFICE OVERSEAS TRADE SERVICES
For: Practical help and support for exporters, contact with trade officials in government offices in the regions and the

DTI's market branch based in London and FCO posts abroad.
Contact: 0171 215 5000

ENGLISH TOURIST BOARD
For: A guide to starting a bed-and-breakfast business.
Contact: Thames Tower, Black's Road, London W6 9EL; tel: 0181 846 9000

ENTERPRISE AGENCIES
For: Advice for start-up businesses including planning and training. For details of your local agency:
Contact: 0121 458 2000, ext. 3955

FEDERATION OF SMALL BUSINESSES
For: Advice on starting a business.
Contact: 32 Orchard Road, Lytham St Anne's, Lancashire FY8 1NY; tel: 01253 720 911

HEALTH AND SAFETY EXECUTIVE
For: Health and safety requirements for businesses.
Contact: 01742 892 345

INLAND REVENUE
For: Tax inquiries.
Contact: Your local tax office, listed in telephone directory under Government Departments

INSTITUTE OF BUSINESS COUNSELLORS
For: Counselling, advice and information on all aspects of starting and running a small business.
Contact: 01423 879 208

INSTITUTE OF CHARTERED ACCOUNTANTS

For advice on choosing an accountant.

Contact: C A Hall, Moorgate Place, London EC2; tel: 0171 920 8100

INSTITUTE FOR COMPLEMENTARY MEDICINE

For: Initial advice on complementary therapies. This is an umbrella group which can direct you to bodies representing a particular discipline.

Contact: Unit 4, Tavern Quay, London SE16; tel: 0171 237 5165

INSTITUTE OF DIRECTORS

For: Advice, information, training, conferences and courses on the needs of a director, partner or sole proprietor of a business.

Contact: 0171 730 4600

INSTITUTE OF TRADING STANDARDS ADMINISTRATION

For: Advice on consumer protection legislation regarding the safety and quality of goods and how to comply with the regulations.

Contact: 01702 559 922

LOCAL AUTHORITIES

For help and advice on local considerations which may affect your business, including bye-laws, planning requirements and public services.

Contact: Under Local Authority in telephone directory

OFFICE OF DATA PROTECTION REGISTRAR

For: Information on data protection registration requirements.

Contact: 01625 535 777

PATENT OFFICE
For: Information on innovations, patents, designs, trademarks and copyright.
  Contact: 01633 813 535

TRAINING AND ENTERPRISE COUNCILS AND LOCAL ENTERPRISE COMPANIES
For: Advice to small businesses on setting up and business planning.
  Contact: Local telephone directory

VOLUNTARY WORK

THE VOLUNTEER CENTRE UK
Dedicated to 'promoting, developing, supporting' volunteering. Offers a free list of local volunteering opportunities in your area, a substantial catalogue of publications on all aspects of voluntary work, and the National Volunteering Helpline.
  Contact: The Volunteer Centre UK, Carriage Row, 183 Eversholt Street, London NW1 1BU; tel: 0171 388 9888; fax: 0171 383 0448; e-mail: voluk(a)mcr1.geonet.de
  National Volunteering Helpline: 0345 221 133

Volunteering in the UK

Your local library is an excellent resource for finding out about volunteering opportunities in your community. The following are a taster of the type of organisations you might be interested in.

THE BRITISH ASSOCIATION FOR COUNSELLING
For advice on becoming a counsellor.
  Contact: 1 Regent Place, Rugby, Warwickshire CV21 2PJ

BRITISH TRUST FOR CONSERVATION VOLUNTEERS

For: Work connected with the protection of the environment.

Contact: 36 St Mary's Street, Wallingford, Oxfordshire OX10 0EU; tel: 01491 39766

CHILDREN'S COUNTRY HOLIDAYS FUND

For: Work supervising small groups of children under the direction of a camp leader at holiday camps.

Contact: 1st Floor Rear, 42–43 Lower Marsh, Tanswell Street, London SE1 7RG

COMMUNITY SERVICE VOLUNTEERS

For: Full-time placements away from home in one of over 1,000 projects for between four and 12 months. Age 35 upper limit.

Contact: 237 Pentonville Road, London N1 9NJ; tel: 0171 278 6601

HOMES FOR HOMELESS PEOPLE

For work alongside the homeless in residential projects throughout the UK.

Contact: 90–92 Bromham Road, Bedford MK40 2QH; tel: 01234 350 853

INDEPENDENT LIVING ALTERNATIVES

For: Work assisting disabled people to live independent lives.

Contact: Fulton House, Fulton Road, Wembley Park, Middlesex HA9 0TF; tel: 0181 902 8998

LOCH ARTHUR COMMUNITY

For: Living and working in the community with mentally handicapped adults, for six months to a year.

Contact: Beeswing, Dumfries DG2 8JQ; tel: 01387 76687

MENCAP HOLIDAY SERVICES
For: Helping on short holidays for the mentally disabled. Also opportunities to assist at a Gateway Club, a leisure time youth club for the mentally disabled, or by working at weekends at a hostel.
Contact: 119 Drake St, Rochdale OL16 1PZ; tel: 01706 54111

THE MONKEY SANCTUARY
For: Assistance at this natural colony of woolly monkeys.
Contact: Looe, Cornwall; tel: 01503 262 532

THE NATIONAL TRUST
For: Assistance with wardening, conservation work.
Contact: Volunteer Unit, PO Box 12, Westbury, Wiltshire BA13 4NA; tel: 01373 826 826

THE OCKENDEN VENTURE
For: Work providing housing for international refugees as well as at reception centres, children's homes and a home for disabled refugees.
Contact: 01483 772 012

QUEEN ELIZABETH'S FOUNDATION FOR DISABLED PEOPLE
For: Help on holidays for disabled adults and children, children in care, the homeless and elderly.
Contact: Holiday Organiser, Lulworth Court, 25 Chalkwell Esplanade, Westcliffe on Sea, Essex SS0 8JQ; tel: 01702 431 725

THISTLE CAMPS (THE NATIONAL TRUST FOR SCOTLAND)
For: Conservation projects.
Contact: 5 Charlotte Square, Edinburgh EH2 4DU; tel: 0131 226 5922

Volunteering Abroad

ARCHEOLOGY ABROAD

For: Work on archeological explorations for specialists and laymen with some experience of digs.

Contact: 31–34 Gordon Square, London WC1H 0PY

BRITISH EXECUTIVE SERVICE OVERSEAS

For: Skilled assistance with overseas projects, drawing on an individual's professional qualifications and experience.

Contact: 146 Vauxhall Bridge Road, London SW1V 2RB; tel: 0171 630 0644

CONCORDIA

For: Environmental and community projects in Europe.

Contact: 8 Brunswick Place, Hove, East Sussex BN3 1ET; tel: 01273 772 086

THE CRANFIELD TRUST

For: Help in times of disaster. Those skilled in engineering, disaster appraisal and languages required. The charity maintains a database of volunteers who may be able to help a wide range of charities.

Contact: 6c Frognal Mansions, 97 Frognal, London NW3 6XT; tel: 0171 794 6487

EAST EUROPEAN PARTNERSHIP

For: Teachers and child-care workers in Poland, the Czech and Slovak Republic, Hungary, Bulgaria and Romania.

Contact: 15 Princeton Court, 53–55 Felsham Road, London SW15 1AZ

INTERNATIONAL COOPERATION FOR DEVELOPMENT

For: Qualified and experienced people to assist on development projects in the Third World on a minimum two-year contract. ICD operates in The Dominican Republic, Ecuador, El Salvador, Honduras, Namibia, Nicaragua, Peru, Yemen and Zimbabwe.

Contact: Unit 3, Canonbury Yard, 190a New North Road, London N1 7BJ; tel: 0171 354 0883

SKILLSHARE AFRICA

For: Health, education, engineering and community development professionals working in Botswana, Lesotho, Mozambique and Swaziland.

Contact: Recruitment/Selection, Skillshare Africa, 3 Belvoir Street, Leicester LE1 6SL; tel: 01533 541 862

VOLUNTARY SERVICE OVERSEAS

For: A wide range of work in developing countries.

Contact: 317 Putney Bridge Road, London SW15 2PN; tel: 081 780 1331

WINANT CLAYTON VOLUNTEER ASSOCIATION

For: Work with children, the homeless, Aids sufferers, the elderly and psychiatric patients in the USA.

Contact: 38 Newark Street, London E1 2AA; tel: 0171 375 0547

EDUCATION

ASSOCIATION OF BRITISH CORRESPONDENCE COLLEGES

For: Distance-learning courses including GCSE, A-level and vocational.

Contact: 6 Francis Grove, London SW19 4DT; tel: 018 544 9559

The ultimate handbook

MATURE STUDENTS' GUIDE

For: Advice on how to get into higher education for the over-21s.

Contact: Trotman and Co, 12 Hill Rise, Richmond, Surrey TW10 6UA

NIACE

For: Their publication *Time to Learn*, which details adult education courses nationwide. Costs £4.25.

Contact: 21 De Montford Street, Leicester EE1 7GE

OPEN COLLEGE OF THE ARTS

For: Distance-learning courses in every area of the creative arts.

Contact: OCA, Houndhill Lane, Worsborough, Barnsley S70 6TU; tel: 01226 730 495

OPEN UNIVERSITY

For: Distance-learning degree courses.

Contact: PO Box 20, Milton Keynes MK7 6YZ; tel: 01908 653 231

PUSH GUIDE TO WHICH UNIVERSITY

For: A full breakdown of universities and their specialisms.

Contact: McGraw Hill Publishers, Shoppenhangers Road, Maidenhead, Berkshire SL6 2QL; tel: 01628 23432